The Now Generation

The Now Generation

DENNIS C. BENSON

JOHN KNOX PRESS
Richmond, Virginia

Scripture quotations are from *The Revised Standard Version of the Bible*, copyrighted 1946 and 1952.

Standard Book Number: 8042-1979-6
Library of Congress Catalog Card Number: 68-25012
© M. E. Bratcher 1969
Printed in the United States of America

Contents

Preface

It was just a small background spot in the large picture. The mod photographer couldn't resist his curiosity as he enlarged the picture again and again. The blowup of his print and mind caused him to be pulled out of himself into even more puzzlement about life and the meaning of the small spot. Michelangelo Antonioni's film *Blow Up* well depicts the progress of this author's quest as he tried to look more closely at one aspect of a subculture in order to understand its relationship to the Christian faith.

This study is not an attempt to capture the whole meaning of rock music or its culture. The task of relating the needs and contributions of youth culture to the Christian faith has only been partially explored here. The reader is invited to look over one person's shoulder and participate in an exercise of listening and understanding.

The aspects of this study which will shock and scandalize some do not apply to every young person. There may not even be one person who is described in the profile suggested in this book. However, the youth culture which emerges from these pages is drawn from what the writer has experienced with young people in many different settings. He is telling it the way he has seen it. The author does not delight in the pain and anguish endured by young people. There is danger and a heavy price to pay for the quest to be human for and with others. The young are paying in many ways.

The author is also convinced that the generations need each

other. However, reconciliation is not possible until each party recognizes the humanity of the other. The uncomfortable experience of passing through these pages may be the first step in the direction of such a dialogue.

Many friends and kindred spirits have participated in this task at different stages of development. Encouragement and advice have been shared freely by these friends and colleagues. On occasion the author has not heeded their wisdom and must accept full responsibility for the final product. Chuck Naspinsky, a friend and graduate student in history, has been a strong influence on the author's understanding of what's happening in contemporary music. Roger Boekenhauer was a colleague during an important period of time when new paths to creative freedom were being discovered.

James Gahagen, William Pennock, David Barnes, Robert McClure, Bob Bonn, and many others have been gadflies to my thinking on this project and critics of my syntax. With good cheer, Josephine Marion, Donna Bortmess, and Marianne Shabatura have reproduced the typescript of the manuscript.

My wife, Marilyn, has been enthusiastic about this project even when common sense would have led less supportive persons to urge alternative activities. As my "significant other," she has been with me through love and critical encouragement.

Words of appreciation are also happily extended to many members of the *now* generation who shared their music and themselves with me.

D.C.B.

1

The Problem: "What's Happening?"

1. Culture and Church: Different Worlds?

> Christianity will go. It will vanish and shrink. I needn't argue
> about that; I'm right, and I will be proved right. We're more
> popular than Jesus now; I don't know which will go first—rock
> 'n' roll or Christianity.[1]

This crackling assessment was not a professional theologian's
radical analysis of the Christian faith in the late 60's. It is a quote
from a popular teenage magazine made by John Lennon, member
of and lyric writer for the Beatles. The reaction to such a candid
remark was immediate in the United States. From the Southern
Bible belt came reports of one radio station after another banning
Beatle records from broadcast. In Birmingham, Alabama, a public
burning of Beatle discs was planned. The South was not the only
area in which there was religious concern and reaction over this
statement of judgment on Christianity from the world of rock
music. In Reno, Nevada, a radio station ran hourly recorded edi-
torials against the English group. Stations in Ohio, New York,
Michigan, Connecticut, and Massachusetts also joined the ban-
the-Beatles protest.

From England came the manager of the group, the late Brian
Epstein, to give press conferences and even an interview on the
Tonight Show to explain the nature of the remarks. There was
some worry about the imminent Beatle tour of many major
American cities. The Memphis, Tennessee, city commission re-
portedly voted unanimously to cancel the Beatles' concert in that

city. Even the stock in Northern Songs, Limited, the publishing house of many Lennon-McCartney songs, dropped on the British stock exchange from $1.40 to $1.26 a share.

This dramatic episode well expresses the existing conflict between the average Christian's view of the rock musician-composer and the validity of his comments on the faith. One radio station manager typified the indignant churchman when he explained his station's banning and the planned burning action: "We just felt it was so absurd and sacrilegious that something ought to be done to show them they cannot get away with this sort of thing."[2] What right has the rock music sector of culture to bring a value judgment against the church of Christ!

The crowd which greeted the Beatles at the London Airport after their successful American tour that August responded for the young generation which is tuned into the rock scene. They shouted: "John, yes! Jesus, no!" In the minds of those "screamies" the church, attuned to another cultural orientation, had made them choose between their world and a faith from an alien culture.

There was a sensitive comment here and there from those close to what's happening in the Christian church supporting what Lennon was saying. Father Thurston N. Davis in *America*, a Jesuit magazine, caught the essence of the Beatle's remark when he wrote,

> It seems to me that Lennon was simply stating what many a Christian educator would readily admit—that Christianity must come alive again in the minds and hearts of the young.[3]

Father Davis and other theologians perceived in John Lennon's words what Miss Cleave, who recorded the original statement, later confirmed, that the writing Beatle has been reading and thinking a great deal about contemporary theology.

Perhaps the thing which most violated the sensitivities of the *other* generation, who resented the statement of the Liverpudlian, was his concluding assessment that "Jesus was all right, but his disciples were thick and ordinary." How "thick and ordinary" the contemporary followers of Christ appear when they react in such a way to the aspects of culture they don't understand!

The relationship between Christ and culture has long occupied the minds of the disciples of Christ. The church seems to have struggled with these two commitments without ever resolving the tension. Often the *other* generation wants to accept the parts of its culture it deems safe and counsels what *Time* magazine has called the *now* generation to reject the aspects which it sees as being evil or different. On close examination it becomes evident that both generations have embraced the world. It is just one generation's ethnocentrism judging the other's alliance.

Some people look at the music and musicians of the contemporary scene and with great assurance claim that no one in his right mind could find "any redeeming merits" in the loud noise, outlandish costumes, incomprehensible lyrics, and wild emotional response. A radio executive has recently instituted a special board of censors to function in a prebroadcast screening of rock music for hidden obscenities in the lyrics. It is reported that he depends on a prostitute and those acquainted with the dark side of life to make sure that nothing wicked slips into the air time.

Evil can be found everywhere. The seminarians were quite shocked by the history professor's analysis of the familiar hymns which had been developed during the religious movement of the late seventeenth century known as "Pietism." The teacher provided the historical context of the church gathered in small gatherings with a strict ethical code which demanded suppression of overt forms of affection. With such a world view as a setting there was written a whole hymnal literature which stresses the worshiper's affectionate relationship with Jesus. This tradition is preserved in much of Protestantism to this day. The individual believer is depicted as walking in lonely places with the Lord or being drawn close to the breast of the Savior. With just a bit of Freudian insight one can quickly discern a deep sexual interest being expressed in this church music. The historian offered the analysis without value judgment. He simply wanted the church to recognize what it is saying.[4] Dietrich Bonhoeffer, the German pastor and theologian who was martyred by the Nazis, was less reserved in judgment when he spoke of this aspect of the church's music:

What rottenness there is beneath all this piety. I tell you I found things that I am almost embarrassed to repeat to you. And all this in hymns too! Yes, that's man! pious man![5]

There is then a similarity between the church's expressed needs in music and that of popular music. There is some material within each of which one is not necessarily proud. However, to make a blanket judgment on the whole of either body of literature or even face each piece with the suspicion of evil intent is senseless. Perhaps for the church and youth there is a healthy need to express even sexuality in their music.

The Christian lives in a definite place and at a definite time. It is a struggle for culturally located man to know who he is in light of the Christ to whom he is committed. The Bible does note the conflict between the world's way and the way of the Christian faith. However, the distinction is not always clear. The Apostle Paul was strongly compelled to work, live, and teach in light of the assurance that these times would pass away. He believed the end was at hand. Yet, even under these conditions we find a man whose message and life were inseparable from his world. He adopted the common language of his day; he tailored his preaching approach to the forms familiar to his audience; and he sometimes used stock cultural morality, and even hymns common to his audience.

A tracing of the history of the Christian tradition through the formation of the New Testament and on into the life of the later church reveals different attitudes being expressed concerning the culture and its forms of art, speech, and music. Those who led the church in the years following the first century were often men trained in the classical background who could not believe that this sensitivity to beauty and philosophy had to be denied when one followed Christ.[6] The authors of the church's hymns throughout the ages have not been able to desert the traditional melodies or tunes often sung at the inns and taverns. Through such aspects of the culture move the worship and faith of the church. The Christian church has a history of meeting the world where it is. The early proclamation of the church made its great

impact on the lives of its people because it was there in the midst
of life. As Christ spoke with the accent and cadence of the
common tongue of his day, so have the bearers of the gospel
been able to use the language and communicational media in
order to be real in the lives of people. Students of Scripture
have recognized in the holy literature of the faith the fabric of
the ancient culture's manner and media. The poetry, images,
hymns, laws, and literature of the common life are used as a
means to witness that God and man are related in the Christ
event.

The Christian faith cannot be separated from its context. Yet,
the tension between divinity and humanity remains. The Christian, who bears the promise that God has become flesh in order
to dwell with man, must struggle to claim the heritage of there
being wholeness even when man's tradition demands fragmentation of culture and church.

2. The Generational War: "The NOW and the OTHER"

The second half of the twentieth century is an age both new
and confusing, just as every age has been. It is an age of two
generations: the *other* and the *now*. Parents complain that their
children are "so different," which often means that they judge
the younger generation as having inferior "tastes" and cultural
attitudes. On the other hand, the young look to the *other* generation as being "uptight downtrippers," that is, fearful people who
have reached the peak of their lives and are now on the way
down. In terms of youth's religious faith there is a real fear on
the part of parents. They correctly perceive that the young
people do not seem to be committed to the organizational church.
Students of culture have a ready audience for endless analyses
of the reasons for the *now* generation's new modes of thinking.
Critics of the church can vaguely say, "What did I tell you
about the need for renewal?" In conversation with college students it is clear that many are not able in good faith to make
a commitment to their parents' church. In many cases they
experience the church negatively passing judgment on all that
is different—on all that comes from the subculture of this age

which the young person chooses. The cultural aspects of the contemporary church chosen and/or preserved by the *other* generation are perhaps not even meaningful to them.

The gentleman at the luncheon table expressed a deep concern over the problems of youth. He wanted to do something for the young people of his church. As the chairman of the Christian Education Committee, he was seeking means to "fix the things that are wrong." His companion at the table mentioned that the young people with whom he had contact had been extremely excited by a popular film produced by a foreign director. The churchman responded that he had seen that film. He had walked out before it was over because it had no meaning for him, and besides it was a "dirty" film. Such is the problem facing the generational gap as it exists in the church. There is little developed ability in the church to understand the idiom of communication and expression which is the language of youth's thinking and feeling. Perhaps if there were a sensitive attempt to learn how to hear what is being said, then the *other* generation could learn what's going on.

The youth of today often find the visible church barren and meaningless in its life, statement of dogma, and witness. Perhaps many will slough off the charge of hypocrisy as the idealism of youth and will view as dangerous a love of the new, fresh, and exciting. However, it was this possibility of change that won so many in the ancient world to the Christian faith.

3. A Perceptual Faith: "With Feeling"

The thrust of theology is passing through a series of convulsions which will not subside for some time to come. The great human pillars of theological thinking from the past do not seem to be "here" at this moment. The *now* generation needs an intellectual and spiritual framework which can be an extension of life experience. This is what the Christian faith must be, but it isn't. So often the drive for renewal within the church is a first-aid campaign to put Band-Aids on a seriously wounded or dying body.

The task before the young and old who are interested in an understanding of the relationship between Christ and this subculture is one of "knowing it like it is." In the teaching of faith to the *now* generation there has often been a concern for the literal content of the Bible. Tests conducted at the college level have shown that there has been a general failure in this goal of conveying facts. It is recognized that a personal manifestation of faith is important in some sort of way. But how? How can one ever evaluate the ability of the members of a generation to know themselves, others, and their place in existence before God? Perhaps the *now* generation even possesses those ideals better than previous generations. However, their expressed faith in these areas seems to have lost continuity with the source, the church. The youth culture is a subculture. It is, however, in an excellent place in which to begin a dialogue of sensitivity in order that we might find what is being said by the Christian faith to today's youth and what the *now* generation is saying to the church.

In our time the people of God need a new understanding of theology as both substance and process. The provocative writings of Marshall McLuhan are most helpful in this quest.[7] He has forcefully reminded us that content and media cannot be separated. In the early tribal setting, interpersonal relationships and all activities of mind and body were transacted on a person-to-person level. With the advent of writing and later printed matter, there came a change in the nature of community life, business, and the transmission of knowledge. A man could individually relate to the printed matter and needed no one else. In the age of electronic media there has been an extension of man's nervous system. The viewer watches television and is "pulled out" by a demand for involvement. As he is forced by the medium to bring meaning to dots on the screen, he rejoins a global tribe in his relationship to others.

The very nature of television as a medium evokes an audience response which may have a greater effect on the viewer than the subject matter of the program itself. There are those who have expressed fear that the mental and physical development of children would be stunted by television exposure. These prophecies have proven to be inaccurate. The children of television are young people who are "tuned in" to the world as no other generation. If it is acknowledged that the screen in the living room or bedroom demands a response of imagination and involvement previously not solicited by the media of the *other* generation, then a communication difficulty between the young and old might naturally be expected. McLuhan describes the involving media as being "cool" in contrast to "hot" media which leave little for the listener or the observer to add. The work of McLuhan is a watershed in our evaluation of change for education and particularly for the church. Most of our education in the public school system, both higher and lower, is based on a "hot" communicational orientation. The church still uses its "hot" means of proclamation in the sermon and Sunday school lecture approaches. We are thus failing to relate to the *now* generation or even those of the *other* generation who are attuned to this age.

Chaplain Carl Burke reports that the young men in prison use the expression "being pulled out" for the theological term "salvation." They understand this key theological word in the sense of a drowning person being pulled out of a creek. Such an insight aptly reflects the *now* generation and its desire "to be pulled out" by that which will give life.[8] The Christian faith has historically been its truest and strongest when the power of God has pulled men out of themselves to feel, in all levels of their being, the needs and gifts of others.

The deep and important meaning of rock music for the *now* generation and the *other* generation's hate or distrust of it indicate that the gap in theology and interpersonal relationships between the generations might be bridged through the acknowledgment that there may be a difference in media orientation. If the change in media orientation is accepted as a possible explanation of the culture's development, a whole new dimension of theology's communication can be explored for the people of God. A new kind of sensitivity to faith and its change of meaning is offered to the church.[9]

Anyone who would have dialogue with the *now* generation
must face a perceptual or sensual aspect of theology. Youth's
orientation asks of the church, "How does the Christian faith
taste? How does it smell, feel, sound, or appear?" No longer
acceptable are answers such as, "It must taste like communion
wafers and grape juice; or it must smell like damp carpeting
and moldy basements; or it must feel to the touch like glass
beads; or it must sound like songs pitched too high for the
men to sing and phrased in language too quaint for this age;
or it must appear only at a given time during the week in the
dress of ladies and gentlemen." The church has often refused
to acknowledge the human senses as the realm through which
man is attuned to his world and his God. The young generation's reaction to the church's sensual constipation is well expressed in Jean-Paul Sartre's play *The Flies*. Electra approaches
Zeus in bitterness:

> Now smell me for a change, smell the perfume of a fresh, clean
> body. But, of course, I'm young, I'm alive—and you loathe
> youth and life.[10]

The church is often represented in our day as hating youth
and its smell, sights, and sounds. The world of today's culture
is exploding with smells, tastes, colors, and action which call
men to be alive. The church comes from another age and yet is
now. This must be so. The message of the Christian faith cannot depend for its essence on the cultural needs of the time.
However, the relationship between the faith of the past and
the life of the present cannot remain broken if there is to be a
living faith.

The perceptual or sensual nature of the Christian life enables
the church to be alert to what is happening. The writer of one
of the Psalms admonished his readers to "taste and see that
the LORD is good" (Ps. 34:8). The faith has been passed on by
those who confidently claimed that they spoke from what they
had seen, touched, and heard (1 John 1:1-4). The senses must
be openly explored as means of understanding, communicating,
and living the Christian faith.

Bishop Pike has spoken of the need to acknowledge *eros* love in the Christian life.[11] The Greek word for love, *agape*, is the familiar term for a love that loves the unlovable. On the other hand, Pike claims that *eros* is the love that loves the lovable. He depicts *eros* love as that which "turns on" one person for another. The Christian life in contemporary society calls man to be "turned on" by that which is lovable and not just by that which is unlovable. More importantly the *agape* love calls the whole man to accept that which is *eros* love for others if there is to be a sharing of what he has to give others and what others have to give him.

There is no place for the naïve assumption that the world gives only that which delights and is good. The youth sub-culture does not have answers for all the needs of life. Ideally, every man would love to be in Ulysses' sandals as he passed the menacing rocks of the Sirens. He was free to hear and behold with all his being the voices and sights of delight, but he remained secured by leather straps with which his crew had bound him to the mast before they put wax in their ears. To reach out with enjoyment to touch, taste, see, and hear the sensual joys of life and not be destroyed by that which is destructive and dangerous is the wish of every man.

If what Professor McLuhan has suggested about media is true, man is forced to recognize the overwhelming world views of this age and yet not be overcome by them. How can the content and media of the good and bad of culture be enjoyed without being unfaithful to Christ? Can the modern Christian Ulysses enjoy both life and faith with security? If McLuhan is correct, then aspects of Christianity which refuse to admit that one must experience the world because it may be dangerous are gone in this era of exploration and mass media. One of the real difficulties of the Christian in the worldly culture is that the media are so inviting. The evening at the movies or coffee house is so much more interesting than a typical church study group. The night out has been chosen. You are relaxed with those you have chosen to be with you. You are looking for entertainment. Through the effective media of song, story, and laughter comes a world of values. Can the inviting forms of the media be separated from their values?

This unanswered question must remain for the reader to face. A wise teacher once counseled, "One cannot do justice to a study unless he loves the material." The present writer comes to the subculture reflected in rock music with excitement, fascination, and a certain love. It is perhaps hard for the reader to do this. The Christian in this new world of perceptual theological concern must allow his *eros* love to accept that which is lovable to those whom he loves. Man is not forced to judge, but only to freely listen, smell, feel, and hear.

4. *The Tuning Process: "Hear, Here"*

Some will say that they cannot hear what is being said in the world of rock music. Such an important admission! What other people are saying with their words, gestures, anger, or even love is frequently not heard. The authors in our study— John Lennon, Bob Dylan, Arlo Guthrie, Paul Simon, and Janis Ian—are saying things important to all. The *now* generation sometimes selfishly hoards the words of its music from the *other* generation who will not take the time or effort to find out what's happening. The tuned-up amplifiers have been used as the reason for not hearing the words of rock music. There seems to be the desire on the part of the performers to remain on the outer fringe of understanding.

The common experience of rock groups at a local television station bears out this difficulty. In one incident the lead guitarist and organ player were very upset over the fact that their equipment would feed directly into the audio man's control unit. They could not control the balance of sound and were disturbed over the possibility that he would mix the electric instruments in such a way as to give the lead singer clarity over the rest of their sound. The young people, however, know the words of this blurred sound experience and desire to keep it this way.

No one can claim that all rock music is of the same quality or value. Some of the material is commercial in the non-creative sense. The lyrics of many songs in the rock genre do not reach the level of the material selected for this study. Just as much of the teaching in the church and the preaching from the pulpit is tasteless and of limited value, so much of the pop scene seems shallow.

There is an important role in the life of man for the trivial and tasteless. Much understanding might be gained by learning to appreciate how man meets some need through his trivia. A theology of culture must focus on all the aspects of society. The good and the bad must both be examined if it is believed that God works through the whole of life. Just as scholars Grenfell and Hunt could find papyri fragments of immeasurable value in the garbage dumps of the ancient Egyptian city of Oxyrhynchus in 1897, so can the sensitive Christian find much of value even in the poorer aspects of culture and its music. Effort must be expended to understand the persons behind even the cheap commercial imitations of the better rock bards.

One of the most important attributes of the current rock music scene is the fact that it reveals the largest songwriter-performer expression in history. Most of the major groups produce all of their own material. There is a desire for creativity and self-expression which says something about the "tuned in" age in which modern man lives.

It is true that the rewards of fame and fortune lure many to join in the race. However, it is interesting to see real development and growth as the groups mature. The close identification of audience with the authors-performers indicates an important need being fulfilled by the current music. It may be another manifestation of hero worship as some critics maintain. However, the qualities in the image or hero tell us something of the needs of this age.

One of the interesting aspects of the rock musician's popularity is the fan mail. The young seek to communicate directly with those whom they respect. Bob Dylan notes that he is most impressed by the nature of the mail he receives:

> They just want to tell me things, and sometimes they go into their personal hang-ups. I like getting them—read them all and answer some.[12]

The lines of communication between the rock poets and their audience often reach the stage of deep identity. This is not the cult of the hero as has often been the case in the past. Certainly, there is the frantic sector which faints at the concerts. However, the more impressive reaction of the young is the intellectual communication between the young person's needs and the composer's ability to understand and respond via the lyrics. Many sensitive college students confess that they are able to listen to their favorite rock writers only occasionally. The concerns of the material are so close to their own thoughts and struggles that they can only take a limited amount of it without becoming completely engrossed. The needs of freedom, honesty, and concern for persons which are typified in many of the teen favorites are not apparently being fulfilled elsewhere.

It is very difficult to participate in a form of art. How does one sympathetically hear what rock music and its generation are saying without investing too much of himself into the experience? What method does one use in the process of having dialogue with the art of another? There is the danger of seeing more theological concern in the lyrics than perhaps the writers intended. Certainly the modern poets and the rock generation are not trying to proclaim a systematic or even explicit theological message as did the fourth-century followers of Arius with their theological songs in the streets of Alexandria.[13] It cannot even be assumed that the fans of this music see the same structure of concern in the lyrics as was intended. Do all the young people even agree with what is being said? Assuredly, the young generation of most churches do know more words of the rock material than they know church hymns. At parties the teeny-boppers often move their lips in time with the records.

The following exercise is simply one person's reaction to what he hears of what is being said. There is much in the music which is not adequately grasped or fully understood. The process of giving one person's encounter with this subculture is shared in order to enable others to begin their own listening. The words of this book about listening cannot take the place of listening to the records themselves. In some cases the author may fall victim to Lennon's reported lament: "I don't want people taking things from me that aren't really me."[14] This study will try not to make the songs say more than was intended. Yet the material stands before the listener, and there is the beholder's right and duty to let it speak to the context of his experience.

It must be underscored that this book does not attempt to survey the complex field of popular music. There are many non-classical idioms which have large followings in our day. It is quite unwise for one attempting to understand the sub-cultures which comprise the general society to make value judgments on whether jazz, folk, country and western, or folk-pop-rock is better or worse than others. They are all different and can only be evaluated and appreciated within their own context. We have chosen the realm of the *now* generation's greatest identification, rock music. There are those who even see a wide range of difference within this general heading.[15]

For some the rock scene is a fast way to make it like a Horatio Alger. The modern-day success uses luck, skill, and magic in place of the hard work and clean living of the hero in the novel series. For the circle of Bards and performers chosen for this study, the world of rock music is a means of being or self-expression.[16] We are basically interested in select performers and who they and their audience are in light of the lyrics.

This is not a book on the "message" of rock music. Such a term comes from the *other* generation or the pre-McLuhan age. Content, media, and self-being are inseparable for performer and audience. As Bob Dylan has stated, the word "message" strikes the young generation "as having a hernia-like sound."[17] He claims that the only people who can deliver "messages" are Western Union boys. Even the cute title of Marshall McLuhan's graphic essay *The Medium Is the Massage* reflects the interrelationship between media as an extension of the creator's and participant's being. There can be no valid dissection of content apart from media.

The kind of communication which develops in the relationship between rock music and the listener is the combination of content and media. The listener participates in the expression of the poet. He may dance, sway, or just feel sounds, words, and emotion. George Orwell comments on flashes of this kind of exchange between creator and audience which occur on occasion in literature, when he writes of James Joyce:

> The effect is to break down, at any rate momentarily, the solitude in which the human being lives. When you read certain passages in *Ulysses* you feel that Joyce's mind and your mind are one, that he knows all about you though he has never heard your name, that there exists some world outside time and space in which you and he are together.[18]

Such a relationship exists between the artist's expression in rock music and the *now* generation. It is our task to experience this world. This is, in a terse sense, the nature of this book. We come to hear what is being said by taking the rock music seriously as an expression of people.

5. Who Are These Prophets? "What Manner of Man Is This?"

THE BEATLES

The announcer on WFMT-FM in Chicago was midway through the weekly entertainment experience which is the "Midnight Special." The late night show is beamed to a select intellectual audience that enjoys the mixture of comedy, folk music, and the unexpected. It is an audience which can respond to an advertiser's select wine special or fill a new integrated apartment complex. Just after the playing of authentic street calls, the host on the show announced, with tongue in cheek, that he would introduce a new sensation from England: The B-e-a-t-l-e-s. He read an article from a London paper about the effect this group was creating with audiences. He then said that he would introduce them to America by playing a cut from the disc he had received from England.

Following the playing of the song, he told his audience that if they were impressed by this sound they could call the station, and if the requests were numerous enough, he would play another. He played another.

The early history of the Beatles' conquest of the world is usually dominated by the screamies and the mass reactions to the sound and personalities. Yet, there is much more to the music and fame of this group. John Lennon, George Harrison, Paul McCartney, and Ringo Starr comprise the combo which has so changed the hair styles and music of our times. From the Cavern, a Liverpool teenage club, to world fame, the four have played a role in England's balance of trade battle and were rewarded amid a heated controversy by being named to the Queen's Honors list as members of the Most Excellent Order of the British Empire.[19] Lennon and McCartney write the bulk of the lyrics and music respectively. George Harrison has written some of their material and has lately led the group to an interest in the music and instruments of India.

John Lennon has not only written the major portion of the songs but is also the author of two books of poetry.[20] In critical reviews he has been placed in the company of Lewis Carroll, James Thurber, and James Joyce as a writer of the fresh and imaginative. In 1964, music critic Peter Schickele lamented that much of this poetic charm was not found in the Beatle material.[21] This judgment would have to be revised in light of the recent directions taken by these amazing and startling persons.

The fame and success of the group have written show business history. From the nights of working in Liverpool for all the soft drinks they could consume to record-breaking income as entertainers, the Beatles have changed the direction of music and youth's culture. Those who are identified by the term "hippy" look to the freedom in the life style and musical sound of the Beatles as the beginning point of their present direction of "dropping out."

Vance Packard is among the students of culture who have tried to explain the Beatles "thing." It is his contention that there are five factors contributing to this craze:

(a) their clean, well-groomed appearance;
(b) an impressive symbol (hairdo);
(c) the subconscious needs of teenager
    girls to mother someone;
(d) a freshness or difference and
(e) parent's annoyance.[22]

He was willing to predict in 1964 that the craze would not last. They are "not really offensive enough to grown-ups to inspire youngsters to cling to them."[23] Time has shown us that their strength has been built upon something much more lasting than mere parental resentment.

With solid fame, the group seems to have moved rapidly ahead with invention and development. Their experimentation with electronic sound and Eastern musical instruments and forms keeps them ahead of the commercial crowd. They also seem to have moved from the simple love lyrics to deep personal concern for people and their problems.

BOB DYLAN

A native of the midwest, Bob Dylan has been able to create or find a world of hardship which was not offered to him in the Hibbing, Minnesota, of his youth. Young Dylan knocked around the country. He ran from something in order to find something else. In the process of discovering new things he found many dreams destroyed and broken. This "wilderness" journey gave him a new perspective about life and people.

After such an apprenticeship about the country, he landed in New York with a world of music and ideas absorbed from the people he met and came to know. People of his travels seem to have impressed him and aided his development more than his brief stay at the University of Minnesota. Successful performances in Greenwich Village soon put the young songwriter and minstrel in the folk scene. The fact that he wrote powerful new material which pulsed with the human need for justice and understanding won followers for him among the people involved in the "movements" for peace and civil rights.

The performing Dylan was part of the draw. With his hair seeking a thousand different directions, he can carry an audience through the pain and sorrow of those burning for meaning and freedom. His guitar and harmonica accompany a voice which is rich in the raw folk tradition of his respected friend, the late Woody Guthrie.

The folk crowd at the Newport Folk Festival booed their hero when he switched to his folk-rock music in 1965. Times were indeed changing. His focus on human suffering has also changed. He is not to be boxed into a "cause" or "movement" classification. He has recently directed his concern for people through songs about man's inner and outer struggle with problems which can be handled only by persons and not "movements." This underground route is the hippy inner-space which so strongly influences the *now* generation's sub-culture. Dylan represents well the flux of the contemporary generation. His late work wanders down a new path which may even be a reaction to the popularity of recent folk-rock music. He again uses the simple guitar, harmonica, and piano. In the album *John Wesley Harding*, he utilizes themes explored in his earlier work. There is an overt religious sensitivity which was less explicit in his folk-rock period.

A poll revealed that Bob Dylan is considered one of the top literary figures in the eyes of students on several campuses.[24] He has been working on a book and may be on the brink of another dimension of his career. Stephen Rose, in an excellent article, notes the marks of a contemporary theological prophet in the works of this man of music.[25] The rock development of electrification of his music has introduced him to an even larger audience. Much of his material has been recorded by other rock groups.

PAUL SIMON AND ART GARFUNKEL

These urbane singers and writers are student types who have made a significant contribution to the musical literature of the *now* generation. Paul Simon writes all the lyrics and much of the music. They have been called a group which is not really folk or rock. They are very much themselves.[26] We include them among those in the rock scene because there is a continuity of subject matter between them and the others under study. Much of their material has been recorded by other rock groups.

There is a quiet reverence about their material which enables the listener to stand in a lonely, difficult world and yet feel that there is something else here. The important contribution of this duo to our study is their more conventional orientation (i.e., college). They, in some sense, represent mainline youths who are perfectly attuned to the same basic trends which underscore the concerns of the other sectors of the subculture. From the college carrel comes the same quest for a meaningful existence in a meaningless society as comes from the pad built of old automobile hoods by hippies on the West Coast. Simon and Garfunkel retain their own identity and yet feed into a mainstream of thought and concern which is sweeping across the *now* generation.

ARLO GUTHRIE

This young composer-performer is new to the music world, but not to the tradition of expressing the hopes and needs of his generation. At twenty, he follows in the footsteps of his late father, the great folk singer Woody Guthrie. The senior singer and poet was an extension of the pain and suffering of depression-ridden America. Arlo captures the throbbing uncertainty, conviction, and impatience of urban youth as they stretch for the 70's.

His first album, *Alice's Restaurant*, includes the sweet and sour of contemporary life. The lengthy and meandering title song about society and war has created a cult of followers. His music and outlook is peculiarly relevant to every young person's plight and hopes.

Arlo can remember well the days of his father's twilight of illness. The long-past day when Bob Dylan dropped by the family home to see his ailing father is still vivid in his memory. His biography has striking parallels to that of Dylan's.

He also tried a few weeks of college life before he hit the road.

The hippy life style currently appeals to him. He views this controversial way of life as being:

> . . . traditional American—the idea that you can do what you want as long as you don't hurt anybody else doing it. Do what you want and don't put anybody else up tight—that's what I'd like to do.[27]

Arlo's thinking about the free life indicates some of the new directions being taken by those who can be intellectually labeled "hippy." He does not live in the city where the tourists and weekend hippies go. The country with the joys of nature is his favorite home.

The hot hand of fame has just begun to touch his life. The complicated business side of the music field with its copyright concerns and inhibiting battle to find privacy has not yet hit the early Guthrie. His ability to view his music as a free happening of spirit and emotion is refreshing. He contributes an uncorrupted voice to the study of youth culture and its people. Although his recorded work is limited at this date, it is certain that he will become a major extension of the *now* generation's most profound concerns.

JANIS IAN

The television camera came in for a closeup on the fifteen-year-old girl as she played her guitar and sang the ballad about the pain and suffering of lovers forced to dissolve their relationship: "I can't see you any more, baby . . . I'm society's child." Such lyrics about heartsick love are not unusual as the concern of a young girl at anytime. One would expect such a performance on a number of teenage dance shows. What made this all so impressive was that the song told the story of a young black boy and a white girl who were in love, but separated by the value judgments of the *other* generation. The girl was not simply performing a song learned from an older protest writer; she had written it herself. The third factor which made this moment extraordinary was that she was performing on a national television show hosted and written by the noted conductor-composer Leonard Bernstein!

Grasping her hand, at the conclusion of the number, he thanked her and predicted that she had a great future in the world of music.

Janis Ian is a New York high school girl who has had the advantage of early training and understanding parents to give her extraordinary talent creative outlet. Her first recorded song, "Society's Child," did not at first get much time on many radio stations because of its controversial nature. Pete Seeger has said that every song is controversial—it just depends before whom you sing it. The *other* generation is shocked by the general content of this young composer-performer's work: alienation, religion, parental influence, and sex. She is of great importance to our study as one speaking from the view of those still close to society's last parental years of influencing the young to conform.

The major influences of the *now* generation's world are presented in her development, though. She is a young, urban woman and yet has so much in common with the others in our study. At present, only a small portion of what will be her major contribution to the world of music is available. However, even with these few songs she adds a great deal to an understanding of rock music and its theology.

More, much more, will the thoughts and writings of these writers be explored in this study. The writers have been picked arbitrarily to represent some of the most important and popular spokesmen for the *now* generation. New things are happening all the time. However, it is important to start somewhere and listen to some of the rock theology as it is perhaps being heard by the youth.

6. A Place to Stand: "How in the World?"

It is reported by tradition that Archimedes boasted that if he only had a place to stand he could move the world. Such a study as this presents a pressing problem which must be faced: Where does one stand or how does the listener approach the material in order to accomplish the task?

A profile constructed by members of the *now* generation has been chosen as a means to look at this subculture through its music. At a conference on the nature of the young generation, a group of students forcefully provided such an outline.[28] This analysis provides a framework in which to stand and study this unsystematic source material. There is always a danger that the chosen structure of a study will predetermine the conclusions. Such subjectivity is present in all research and must simply be accepted and the needed correction of balance provided by the subjectivity of the reader. There are six convenient points under which our material may be grouped on the basis of this profile:

(1) The *now* generation is irreverent about the sacred of the past.
(2) The *now* generation is humanistic and concerned with the meaning of personhood.
(3) The *now* generation relishes personal experience which is spontaneous.
(4) The *now* generation rejects the puritan work ethic.
(5) The *now* generation rejects war.
(6) The *now* generation rejects the structure of society as it tends to dehumanize people.

Such an outline does not completely fit each individual writer or even each young person. However, this profile adequately captures the major thrusts of our time.

2

The Irreverent Generation:
"Ban the Bible" (From a Bathroom Wall)

During the Christmas vacation the *now* generation college student impatiently tries to make the *other* generation parent understand his rejection of a view which had been sacred in his family life. The mother and son become entrenched in their respective positions even more stubbornly. Finally, with the mother in a near state of tears and the son overcome by the futility of not being able to communicate, he puts his hands on his mother's shoulders and bewilders her even more by saying, "Don't worry. The Jefferson Airplane loves you." How impertinent such a response seems to be to some! Is this any way for a son to speak to his mother? It is a typical example of the "cultural nag" between the old and young and the deep frustration a lack of communication creates.

Every society has that which is reverent, holy, or sacred to it. An act of reverence is to have "profound respect mingled with love and awe (as for a holy or exalted being or place or thing)."[1] In the past almost every age and every people seem to invest a need for something that is protected from the disrespect and profanity of daily existence. The way a culture or subculture seeks that for which it has profound respect is the dynamic process of rediscovering the holy, sacred, or reverent object, place, or tradition. As man desires to have the holy or reverent aspect of his life meaningful to him, he finds that he must discover it anew for himself.

The process of acknowledging a holiness in this age may be accomplished through redefinition which actually changes the nature of the sacred while keeping the form which is familiar. Sometimes this is done without the change being acknowledged. For example, man in a certain age may develop a method of allegorically interpreting a sacred book which has always been literally understood in the past so that it might have some meaning of reverence in the current irreverence of human existence. The resulting influence on human life from such a method of interpretation may be quite different, but father and son still have the same holy book.

There often is a bit of dishonesty in the task of changing the holy or being irreverent with the past. The aged woman proudly tells about her daughter who smokes, but will not smoke in front of her. "She knows how I feel about smoking and she thinks I don't know that she does. I hope to catch her sometime and give her a good lecture about this wicked practice." How many parents or older relatives of *now* generation people refrain from smoking openly to protect the sacred or reverent views of a parent or grandmother? In this case, the sacred law about smoking has been rendered meaningless by the current *other* generation, but a deceit is allowed to keep the elders from knowing about the process of irreverence that has taken place.

The age of electronic media with its ability to relate all parts of the culture into one tribal family has accelerated the process of irreverence. In many cases, the old passes away before the new value or holiness has been able to make an impact. Some have seen in this rapid change a new process of secularization or irreverence which will eventually replace the ancient task of man having to create or find a "holy other" or sacred dimension outside of this experience.[2]

The process of religious irreverence is not new to the Christian tradition. In the day of Christ there were many who saw in his message an overturning of the past's sacred values. Even the church's ability to preserve the tradition of Jesus as having continuity with the Old Testament cannot disguise the aspect of Christ's life and mission which led some to believe that, as Paul later expressed it, "the old has passed away, behold, the new has come" (2 Cor. 5:17).

The awareness of the process of irreverence is very threatening to man at any time. The fact that it is now so clearly present makes the crisis seem overwhelming. Whether this swift-moving process will bring new vistas of human development remains to be seen. However, fear is overcome if it is acknowledged that the process of irreverence about the holy of another day is the necessary bridge of continuity between the past and the future. There are at least three areas in which the *now* generation is speaking in terms of its irreverence: religion, the *other* generation, and nationalism.

1. Religion

The *other* generation's understanding of the holy in religion as being static has often been combined with a picture of authority which calls for fear on the part of the young. Jean-Paul Sartre, in *The Flies*, bitterly comments on such a view through the words of a female character who responds to her son's cry that he is frightened by the community penance ceremony in ancient Greece: "And so you should be, darling. Terribly frightened. That's how one grows up into a decent, god-fearing man."[3] This kind of fear and authority is gone, and the religious irreverence of the *now* generation is quite outspoken and striking. One is amazed both by the radical nature of the act of religious irreverence by the *now* generation and by its continuity with the past. On the one hand, we must contend with John Lennon's put-down of religion and the wild Beatle remarks which jar the holiness of yesterday's values. There is also Bob Dylan with his long hair which never seems to have been touched by a comb. We have Donovan with his clothing from another age worn in such a way that it offends that age.

There is also another aspect to the problem. John Lennon can assert, "I believe Jesus was right, Buddha was right, and all of those people like that are right. They're all saying the same thing—and I believe it."[4] The writing Beatle contends that the people who call themselves Christians have failed to listen to the words of

Jesus. They have substituted prayers and religious forms as holy acts in the place of what Jesus was calling them to do. This irreverence toward yesterday's religion in our day is reflected in "Eleanor Rigby." It is the story of a lonely girl who only picks up the rice of other people's weddings in the church. The ministry of the church is seen in these terms:

> Father McKenzie writing the words
> of a sermon that no one will hear,
> no one comes near.
> Look at him working,
> darning his socks in the night
> when there's nobody there . . .
> what does he care?[5]

The lonely girl dies in the church building and an unattended funeral is conducted by the priest:

> Father McKenzie wiping the dirt
> from his hands as he walks from the grave,
> no one was saved.[6]

Here is a naked statement on the holiness of the past not speaking to the needs of the present.

Paul Simon makes a statement of how the past is not holy to the present in different terms. In his reverent song "Blessed," he points to how the religion of the past can meet the needs of the present if radically translated into contemporary concerns. Building upon the Sermon on the Mount he captures the present context of where holiness or the new reverence must be manifested. The Lamb of God bled for the heartless rejection of men who thought themselves holy. God's blessedness must also then be with those who this day suffer while being the object of everyone's scorn. Simon is able to weave the suffering of contemporary men into the person of the forsaken Christ. The edge of irreverence about the traditional religion is still here, but the reverence for religion as radical concern for people is affirmed.

In other verses the dope pusher and LSD users are included among those to be blessed. The past focus of reverence is underscored as being of questionable value when Paul Simon writes about the state of uneasiness induced by the religious trappings of the past's reverence. The stone buildings, leaded glass windows, and structured liturgy of unfamiliar words brings anxiety to the troubled and suffering of this age. This song expresses the irreverent contention that God as reflected in contemporary establishment religion has forsaken those among whom holiness is needed and being found. In the songwriter's statement we find the cheap criminal, the prostitute, and the shapely chick among those who are the object of the new holiness's blessing.

There is a heightened religious irreverence in the Simon song "A Poem on the Underground Wall," which relates the tale of a man's lonely quest to write a four-letter term on a subway wall. The task is undertaken in terms of a religious pilgrimage. The subway train in passing emits a liturgical rhythm and the underground fugitive handles his writing instrument like prayer beads. The contrast of the irreverent quest described in the reverent terms of the past is a powerful statement on secularization. Is the new holiness really what the past thought of as obscene? It is easier to grasp this process of making the new reverence through an apparent irreverence in the Simon-Garfunkel recording of the "7 O'Clock News/Silent Night." The singers reverently sing the traditional Christmas carol while a voice reads the evening news. The voice slowly becomes louder until finally news of the death of eight nurses, civil rights injustice, and war casualties overtake the hymn of peace and holiness.

Paul Simon's ability to recognize the reverent and meaningful is reflected in his wonderment and respect for the underlying principal of the hippy movement: "It is 'love your neighbor.' It worked 2,000 years ago. It will work again."[7]

Bob Dylan also reveals a strong concern for this theme of religious irreverence. In "Highway 61 Revisited" the mountain top of holiness where Abraham was tested becomes the mainstream of Highway 61. Moving from the story of Abraham and Isaac, the writer includes the new holy company of the poor, the "fence," the unfaithful, and the gambler. Here is the where and who of the chosen people in the context of a gutty existence.

In the "Ballad of Hollis Brown" Dylan tells the tale of a destitute family of seven caught in the depths of despair. The father is finally driven to kill his wife, his children, and himself. In one verse Dylan speaks of the man's faith and its failure to help him at this brink of destruction. The man opens his heart in one last plea for God to send him a friend. The negative answer such a man receives seems to equate money with friends. If you lack one, you do not have the other. Old-time religion is for old-time people with money.

In "With God on Our Side" Dylan attacks society's claim that the holiness of their God can justify everything. This reverence of the past becomes a partner for war and destruction at the hands of the *other* generation. The challenge to the old reverence is thrown down before the *other* generation. If the many words of faith have any meaning then there would be no war. The Lord of love and peace would stop killing if he were with our side.

Reference to the popular religion of reverence is reflected as being invalid once again in "Bob Dylan's 115th Dream." In a mock retelling of American holiness he expresses the lack of this reverence's effect on the moral disposition of the people. A stranger or immigrant appeals to a good American and asks for hospitality. The angry citizen is immediately hostile and threatens the visitor in Bob Dylan's dream. The citizen offers to inflict bodily harm to the traveler when a mention is made that Jesus also had been refused hospitality. The American cannot see any continuity between one who is homeless and the Son of Man. Religion as uptight fear has no place in the contemporary youth's discovery of man's need for others.

In "It's Alright, Ma" Dylan comments on the society and its gods. He states that the holy and secular societies do not really relate to the reverence of the past. The society plays with gods of plastic in such a way that the sacred is only man's game of holiness as an extension of himself.

The *now* generation sees in the religious holiness of the past an irreverence which is simply a meaningless exercise of words for the *other* generation. Dylan attacks this use of holiness in "Who Killed Davey Moore?" The boxer whose fists killed an ailing opponent, Davey Moore, is depicted as vainly attempting to use his idea of holiness to rescue him from responsibility by claiming that it must have been God's will.

The process of shaking off the past reverence in the quest for a new meaning of the holy is painful to those dedicated to the past. However, the religious irreverence of this generation has its positive affirmation. This can be more readily understood in the discussion of the humanistic aspect of this generation and its music which appears in a later chapter.

2. *The Other Generation*

The *other* generation was raised on the biblical commandment to honor one's father and mother. The thrust of this sacred assumption has been worked into the very fabric of society since the days of the home industry in early America. The church has supported the subordinate position of the young, and at one time had a struggle to recognize the youth as a person. Horace Bushnell, Christian educator, left the contribution that the young should not be looked upon as unredeemed sinners waiting for conversion. The philosophy of Christian nurture as the church's ministry to the young created a new sensitiveness to the needs of children. During the first two decades of this century the social gospel crusaders fought for child labor laws and basic health standards for food and milk to give the young a chance to live.

Some in our day will be sure that the process has gone too far. "The youth have everything and we of the *other* generation have no rights." It is disturbing to such people to view the stratum of tradition in the New Testament which preserves Christ's attitude toward the family. At one point Jesus is told that his family awaits him outside of the meeting. He responds by naming as his true family those who hear the word and respond (Mark 3:31-35). The eschatological call to leave the revered family behind to die and bury itself in order that a person may strike out to preach the gospel in the world is not viewed comfortably by those who have their pride bruised by love of the irreverence of the young toward the old (Matt. 8:21-22).

Christ might even set child against parent (Matt. 10:34-39). The Nichols and May comedy routine "Mother and Son" well captures the pain of longing for respect in the lives of the old and the battle for independence in the lives of the young. The mother calls her rocket-engineer son to demand his concern. He resists her need for attention until she unmercifully nags him about his failure as a son. At one point in the conversation she tries to excuse her worry and frustration by saying, "I am a mother." The son tersely responds, "Well, that's the *thing*."[8]

A mother tearfully tells a friend that her nice daughter learned in college to hate her mother! Again, the actual encounter of the two generations with their different orientations makes the process of irreverence seem more disrespectful than it actually is. The parent discovers that by the Thanksgiving break his freshman son or daughter is "different"—if the school is good. The student now undertakes the task of examining the sacred cows of his family, a process which is threatening to the family. They worry about the young person, and they quietly feel uncertain about themselves under the probing of the junior scholar. It is time for communication and acceptance of the fact that there is a changing of the holy.

The young person faces a difficult time in his search for a new understanding of himself in relationship to his family. When the truth of parental limitation is discovered by the young, they struggle to be honest. The *now* generation cannot accept the phony irreverence of their parents as they continue to hoodwink their parents in full view of the *now* generation. Anne Frank, the young girl who hid with her family in Nazi-occupied Holland, aptly expresses the pain of such honesty. Her mother came to say evening prayers at her bedside and was told by her daughter that she was not wanted in such a capacity:

> Mummy got up, paused by my bed for a moment, and walked slowly towards the door. Suddenly she turned around, and with a distorted look on her face said, "I don't want to be cross, love cannot be forced." There were tears in her eyes as she left the room. . . . I can only feel sorry for Mummy, who has now had to discover that I have adopted her own attitude. For myself, I remain silent and aloof; and I shall not shrink from the truth any longer, because the longer it is put off, the more difficult it will be for them when they do hear it.[9]

How can love and truth be combined to ease the transition between the old reverence and the new?

John Lennon beautifully describes the pain of the child turning from the home. In "She's Leaving Home" a girl is seen slipping down the stairs of her home to go alone into the world. She is crying. The parents awaken and discover the desertion and immediately lament:

> She (We gave her most of our lives)
> is leaving (Sacrificed most of our lives)
> home (We gave her everything money could buy)
>
> . . . . . .
>
> Daddy our baby's gone.
> Why would she treat us so thoughtlessly
> How could she do this to me.
> She (We never thought of ourselves)
> is leaving (Never a thought for ourselves)
> home (We struggled hard all our lives to get by)[10]

The child is running against the reverence for her family. She is escaping because the holiness has been based on an obviously selfish motive of the parents. Whether such selfishness actually exists in most families or not, many young people feel it does and that impression is not corrected by their experience during the time of conflict.

The college age young person is often caught in an act of irreverence to the family when he expresses his concern for people. For instance, the white college student has been tutoring the ten-year-old black boy and it has been going very well. The tutor has found great meaning and self-understanding in this relationship. The teachers at the grade school claim they can see a definite improvement in the young boy's work since the tutoring began. The college student is obviously proud of this work as he talks to the professor. When asked what his parents think about his accomplishment, the student blushes and admits that he has not told them. "They don't understand about these things and would force me to stop. They tell me not to get involved." Reverence for the family does not have any meaning on such a false basis.

Most of the rock music concerning the family is irreverent only in a generalized sense. The lyrics express first critical awareness of their parents. They often discover in the mother and father representatives of those who sold out ideals and meanings of life for security. It is interesting to see in the work of Janis Ian, the sixteen-year-old writer and performer, a cutting edge of reaction concerning the family which is not present in the other writers. She speaks from the heart of a youth still caught directly in the family situation as a subordinate. Her material is not autobiographical, but rather typical of the younger youth's fight to build a new reverence. In "Janey's Blues" the story of an unwanted child in the affluent society is movingly depicted:

> Hey, Janey's just an accident,
> Fatal mistake on the day after Lent,
> And her parents always say, "We don't need you today
> And we expect just the same."
>
> .   .   .   .   .   .
>
> Her Mother plays on the golf course ev'ry day
> Another daddy sits at home and plays with the maid.[11]

The parents just use Janey as an excuse for not getting a divorce. They give her the world in things but not in love and acceptance. The story line is not that unusual. In some sense it cuts at the heart of the American parent who does not provide a basis for family honor and respect by the young.

Miss Ian uses the folk tradition in her beautiful song "Hair of Spun Gold." The poetic power does not weaken the raw story of exploited youth at the hands of parents who rob their children of childhood. The song is the saga of life, love, and age from five through twenty-one years. At ten the joy of childhood is put away:

> My life, it did change again.
> I threw away all my childish toys
> And worked on getting noticed by the boys.[12]

When the girl is sixteen, the mother of the story permits her matchmaking instincts to have their way:

> He held my hand in marriage
> And when sixteen years of age,
> In my arms I held my babe.[13]

The bitter judgment of youth on this aspect of the family is balanced so beautifully as the girl says:

> Now I'm looking down on my child
> I swear she'll have the time
> there'll be time to love
> there'll be time to learn
>   for childish memories she won't yearn.
> Time to laugh and find time to play;
> She won't have to throw her toys away.[14]

The irreverence of this song is cast in the light of seeking a new reverence for the family. Miss Ian is not attacking the concept of the family or family life. She rather affirms positively that she and the rock generation must work to create a meaningful parent-child relationship.

The parent who perverts sex for the young is another irreverent commentary on what happens to some young people in our society. "(Too Old To) Go 'Way Little Girl" is a biting attack on mothers who do not acknowledge the sexual awakening of youth:

> Don't go out in the park, little girl,
> You know boys, they're all the same.
> Stay inside after dark, little girl;
> A boy wants just one thing.
> Don't talk about sex; you might get hexed.
> God will punish you for your dirty mind.[15]

Their means of dealing with sex is to feed a personal fear or delight by painting pictures of terror or religious fear for the young son or daughter. The destructive results find the young person driven to greater distortions than his natural desires would have led him if nurtured with love and understanding.

In "Society's Child" youth's freedom to love and understand

others across racial barriers is destroyed by the parent who warns, "But, honey, he's not our kind."[16] The parent is the supportive agent of prejudice and hatred. Youth must be irreverent to this kind of relationship.

Bob Dylan offers an explanation for what is happening in the apparent irreverence of our times in his popular song "The Times They Are A-Changin'." He pleads with parents to withhold judgment concerning things they really can't comprehend. The sensitivities and ideals of the young are beyond the parental control. A new path has been forged for those ready for change. Others will be passed by if they can't move with the times.

Just as the *other* generation has trouble in this relationship between the changing times, so does the young person. There is a devilish edge of satisfaction in "blowing minds" of the *other* generation. The parents respond on cue and are so often overcome by the shoes worn without socks or the hair carefully groomed to look unruly. In the song "I Shall Be Free No. 10," Dylan writes of a young person's desire to invade a conservative country club with his hair down to the ground and a liberal publication under his arm, in order to explode a few conservative minds. The young person is sensitive enough to know just what will upset the mind-set of the adult. The whole realm of political opinion has a disturbing effect on the old person. The young enjoy the excitement of trying on different political stances. Such ideological hopscotch seems very irreverent to the parent.

Youth and their parents are limited by the belief that reverence for the family must be expressed in the ways prescribed by the past. The parent often demands that honor be expressed through conformity to the past's life styles. John Lennon casts this point nicely in "Your Mother Should Know":

> Let's all get up and dance to a song
> That was a hit before your Mother was born
> Though she was born a long time ago
> Your Mother should know—your Mother should know.[17]

The youth does not always understand that his natural quest to find a new reverence for the family will change the past but

need not be judged as failing to honor his parents. The generations need each other for continuity and what they have to say.
Perhaps the greatest true reverence the younger generation could
express for those who gave them life is to bravely strike out
on this quest for the new, without anger or guilt. The parents
have then given them a sense of reverence for the family which
should be passed on—the substance and process of reverence as
"becoming" and not an empty form of acceptance. The rock
music of our time does not try to "get" the parental generation.
The rock musicians may "bug" parents a bit as the Beatles in
their innovations tended to do in the early days, but the songs
often reflect a quest for an understanding of what can be meaningful about the family now.

3. *Irreverence Toward Nationalism*

The teacher dramatically stopped his lecture on the meaning
of symbolism and its power upon those for whom it is meaningful
by slowly taking an American flag from his desk. He displayed
it for all in the high school classroom to see. Dropping it to the
floor, he astonished the students by standing on it! The astonish-
ment of the school, parents, and community people followed.
At an after-school assembly the ex-marine explained to the students what he was trying to do in this act of teaching. Many
people are worried about nationalism among the young. They see
and are made aware of youth's unrest over national foreign policy
through that extension of our nerve system, television. Many
members of the *other* generation were disturbed by the Confession of Faith adopted by the United Presbyterian Church in the
United States of America. It could be dangerous for Presbyterians
to ascribe to a confession which proclaims: "God's reconciliation
in Jesus Christ . . . requires the pursuit of fresh and responsible
relations across every line of conflict, even at risk to national
security, to reduce areas of strife and to broaden international
understanding."[18]

The global tribe which has been re-established by mass media
has contributed to the *now* generation's international sensitivity
which threatens an older national parochialism. The *now* genera-

tion can understand the theological call to men of faith to make the commitment to the family of man before commitment to the customs, laws, and traditions of a geographical unit, the nation.

Rock music has an international character which enables a cultural exchange to become so fluid that the *now* generation as a subculture has more in common throughout the world than do the different generations within any given country. Lenny Bruce, the late comic, expresses this irreverence for the old nationalism by affirming his love of democracy. This commitment to country does not encourage him to purchase ads on Radio Free Europe. This kind of patriotism does not seek to convert the world to our form of government. There are no good or bad judgments to make on a country. The patriot simply loves this America. He can allow the socialist or communist to like his land. Bruce reminds us that no person has a right to judge another country as long as schools can be closed to prevent integrated education in our land. It may be added that the patriot also is restricted in any such temptation to moralize as long as assassins can destroy a John F. Kennedy or a Martin Luther King, Jr.

The youth of today are seeking a new reverence for their country which must again pass through the act of irreverence in order to find meaning. As the sectionalism of America's past (colony vs. colony; East vs. West; North vs. South; now, urban vs. rural) underwent a process of secularization or irreverence, so it is proper that there be a revolution against the reverence for nationalism. Bob Dylan classically states this in his biting song "With God on Our Side." He speaks about the death of the past's reverence for religion and nationalism. The history text may still tell of our glorious victories. However, the Indians fell from the white man's bullets, and we claimed that it was God giving such strength. Dylan's song recites the killing by people with God on their side in the Spanish-American War, the First World War, the Second World War, and now the cold war. A people with such a reverence for a national god claim his favor as they teach their children to hate the Russian people. Such a pattern of nurtured distrust and fear is part of a nation who accepts God as justifier of all policy.

In "Bob Dylan's 115th Dream" a picture of a passing nationalism is depicted. Through the idiom of satire and dream he tells of coming to America as an explorer and finding false patriots and the contemporary harshness that is in this country. The dreaming Dylan sails away at the end of the song to leave nationalism to others. His fantasy journey of discovery encouraged him to reject any relationship with this kind of land. He wished others lots of luck in such a hostile country.

The irreverence for the country which is often found among those seeking a basis of new holiness in country, in justice, in dignity of purpose, and in concern for the needs of the world is expressed in a love song from Dylan's pen, "Quit Your Low Down Ways." This poetic piece reveals a cynicism about symbols such as the national Capitol which seem depleted of meaning to most people.

In the midst of this irreverence one catches a lyric which opens up the new holiness sought by the younger generation. In the song "Let Me Die in My Footsteps," Dylan captures the beauty of the American West which compels man to love his country and life. Man's soul can't resist the beauty of America's land. This love of country is patriotism which pleads for the human option of dying a natural death and not one beneath nuclear ash. This is an affirmation for life as part of one's nation. It is a nation which is not simply hidden in a big flag. The *now* generation must manifest the attributes which are the basis of a peaceful and just people living for people among people.

When the land access which connected the Rock of Gibraltar to Spain was closed, it is reported that a small group of British subjects gathered at the checkpoint solemnly sang "Yellow Submarine." This humorous song written by John Lennon pokes a bit of irreverent fun at a narrow nationalism. It is the simple story of escapism beneath the sea in a yellow submarine. Everyone has all they need in a colorful fantasy world of sky and sea with a chosen "nation" of neighbors. The Beatles create their new nationalism and process of irreverence in England on a different level from that chosen by Dylan. The constructive side of this new nationalism of the rock poet and his following can be seen in the issues of war and rebellion.

Irreverence then is the process of making the holy of yesterday meaningful for today's demands and needs. The manifestation of changing values and faith has always been painful and frightening. In our day youth's irreverence is an extremely obvious rebellion. The speed, style, openness, and broad range of this changing of the past's holy tend to nurture a hostility in the *other* generation. The fact that the youth subculture is so devoted to this task of finding a meaningful holiness is the one hope that the Christian church has to develop a living faith.

The Humanistic Generation: "Man Alive!"

It was Easter morning and the lonely sculptor started his pilgrimage of witness to the humanity of Christ's suffering on the cross. For months he had gathered the scrap materials of human existence which collect at every time—whether in the smoldering refuse of the valley of Gehenna outside ancient Jerusalem or in a New York City junkyard. With loving care, the artist had constructed a Christ and his cross. The sculpture breathed with the passion of death and the affirmation of reality for the present state of man. He finally positioned the cross in Manhattan's Tompkins Square Park where those going to church in the early morning might confront the reality of the price paid for their gift of love from God.

During the morning crowds gathered and strange things happened. They muttered with anger and hostility over the stark depiction of the man for others. At last a man came and knocked down the cross and ripped from the body of Christ the piece of metal representing a symbolic penis. Christ disemboweled, castrated, dehumanized by the faithful![1] This actual event stands so uncomfortably symbolic of the contemporary church as viewed by a wide sector of the *now* generation. Christ's humanity is denied to those who long for the reality of God become flesh for man here and now.

It has been a combination of reasons which has forced man in the history of the Christian faith to struggle with the problem of Christ's humanity and the church's view of human life. The theology of the medieval period could focus on the problems of the spiritual and leave their Christ on a mountain top, because the state of man's existence was uncertain, fearful, and filled with ignorance. Jean-Paul Sartre attacks this aspect of Christian history in his play *The Flies*, when he has Zeus observe, "Their eyes [people's] are so intent on me that they forget to look into themselves."[2]

The Christian humanitarian concerns of the early years of the twentieth century can be linked to the confidence in progress in all human endeavor. Things were beginning to move on the human scene, and the human Christ seemed relevant to the needs of the times. The wars of this century have destroyed this social gospel thrust. It was replaced for a while with emphasis on the meaning of the Word of God. There has been, however, in the 60's a rebirth of optimism in some circles of theology. It is not the optimism of the first naïve flush of what the new industrial age could do for man. The new humanistic approach to the Christian life is built upon man's new awareness of the complexity in this time of the bomb, the pill(s), the digit identity, the inner space of the self, and the death of everything. Man has had his eyes opened and now must become fully human in the world. Whether the prospect of man set free will lead to the golden age of true man remains to be seen. However, it cannot be denied that the culture is caught in a period which is seeking to recover its humanity.

The Christian can find good precedence for man being concerned with life in the created order. The Incarnation, as a theological statement of God's love for the world being so acute that he emptied himself to become flesh, has validity for those in this revolution. A wide spectrum of people from the current culture has seen in the human figure of Jesus Christ something relevant. A comic, Lenny Bruce, could say,

> I really loved Christ and Moses. I related very strongly to them because it seemed to me that I thought so much like them in so many ways. They had a deep regard for education and they continually gave, with no motivation other than to give.[3]

Even to the hippy, Jesus is "groovy." John Lennon speaks with reverence about the human Jesus, "I believe what Jesus actually said—the basic things he laid down about love and goodness—and not what people say he said."[4]

In the past, man felt the daily threat to his humanity from many sources and could do nothing about it. Today man is much freer to direct the destiny of his health, work, education, and pleasure. He is, therefore, concerned with his humanity. The humanity of Christ, then, stands before our age as a means or medium of communication by which the meaning of it all can be known. Christ is the "fleshing out" of God's love for man here and now. Such an incarnation of God for man is, however, only infrequently manifested in the visible church of our day.

It is true that at the hands of modern man the Christ of Scripture takes surprising shapes. However, the confusing picture of the man Christ has taken on a new flexibility for Christians in our day. Critical studies by students of Scripture have revealed that the church has preserved in the New Testament literature a picture of Christ which seems to be several different pictures overlaid on top of one another. A person can construct one biblical pattern of Christ's reaction to the world only to find another which seems to run against it. Such a new understanding of the New Testament as containing many traditions invites the Christian to the exciting task of seeking to discover the "real" Jesus. It also enables the church to acknowledge that it must seek a fresh understanding of humanity in our age and thereby join the age in its most important concern.

The rock generation places a major focus of its thinking and action on the humanistic aspect of existence. This is perhaps natural for the young. They are freshly aware of their senses as they fight pimples. They know their bodies as they fight to keep a good figure, and they see themselves as objects of interest and admiration by the other sex. The young know the importance of interpersonal relationships as they seek that guy or that girl. The realms of skills, plans, and a future are close to their personhood. The perspective of this generation gives them a deep interest in that which can be felt, tasted, seen, and heard. Theology in our time must struggle with this humanistic sensitivity of the *now* generation, aid in its development, and participate in its exploration.

In order to understand what the *now* generation is saying about the humanistic quest, it is most useful to recognize youth's desire to discover the meaning of being a person in the world. As one looks closely at this humanistic emphasis or the concern for persons, it is obvious that there are several convenient categories under which one might approach an attempt to listen: (a) love, (b) interpersonal relationships in general, and (c) a zest for life.

1. Love: "You Turn Me On"

Poems and songs of love have been part of man throughout history. One of the books in the Old Testament is as beautiful and as sensual a love poem as has been written. The Song of Solomon, also called Canticles or Song of Songs, has been looked upon with embarrassment by religious types in both the Jewish and Christian traditions. For example, an ancient rabbi explained away its obvious sensuality by allegorically interpretating the lover's description of the beloved's body. Not wanting to take literally the beautiful verse "Your two breasts are like two fawns, twins of a gazelle, that feed among the lilies" (Song of Sol. 4:5), the ancient teacher interpreted "Your two breasts" as referring to Moses and Aaron! Christian exegetes have also often bypassed the overt love song to find allegorical meanings concerning the love of Christ for his church. If the human love of a person's wholeness—mind, personality, and body—is literally accepted, then this descriptive love poem can be appreciated for its beauty and charm.

Denis de Rougemont has ably depicted the process of reorientation in the Western world from the refreshingly human love to the courtly romance from the Middle Ages.[5] The bitter sweetness of suffering under a love which is distant, removed, or impossible is the fate of the courtly lover. "The Rules of Courtly Love" seem, in part, to be the order of the day in much of the contemporary romance in films, television series, and women's magazines. Andreas Capellanus, writing in the twelfth century, offers these rules:

> xiv. The easy attainment of love makes it of little value; difficulty of attainment makes it prized.
> xvi. When a lover suddenly catches sight of his beloved his heart palpitates.
> xx. A man in love is always apprehensive.
> xxii. Jealousy, and therefore love, are increased when one suspects his beloved.
> xxiii. He whom the thought of love vexes eats and sleeps very little.[6]

Such guidelines seem to be axiomatic in our day among many people. Such an understanding of love as a "feeling of pain" and not commitment founded upon a foundation of relationship which grows and develops is often reflected in the shallow romantic songs chosen by Christian couples for their wedding ceremonies. The popular entertainment and advertising of our time continues this tradition of a romantic love which is lacking in the humanistic qualities of an interpersonal commitment which recognizes and relishes in the sensual joys and daily difficulties of becoming persons to each other and in the presence of each other.

The musical picture of love among the youth of our day is a mixed bag of viewpoints. There is the strong theme of unrequited love which is the tragedy of the young in their awareness of suffering from the broken relationship. The current generation is struggling to recover the sensual level of the love relationship which has often been repressed or corrupted at other times in our history. This often obscures a basis of relationship which transcends the dangerous superficialities of "romantic" love.

Paul Simon's tender love ballads pulsate with the romantic longings of yesterday's popular music; yet he expresses an undercurrent of concern for persons. In "For Emily, Whenever I May Find Her" he depicts a girl of his dream. Emily is captured in dreamy images of fine cloth and absorbing colors. Her presence is an experience which immerses one in an imaginary rain. From this traditional view of the beloved, he recalls in the next verse how she came running to him as a spirit in the flesh, colored with the excitement of the evening. His dream is of walking—of holding her hand. And then the last few lines move from dream to reality. The lover awakens from his dream fantasies to thankfully realize that the girl of his life sleeps peacefully beside him. She is there. She is real. He tearfully kisses the hair of this sleeping love.

Paul Simon again demonstrates the power of evoking love in humanistic terms which is touched with something that transcends the crude in "Wednesday Morning, 3 A.M." He expresses the humanistic love of a girl through the use of sensual comprehension. He hears the breathing of one who sleeps at his side. The rhythm and beat of love's form is there to experience in the silence of the night. Simon accepts the observable and realistic as the means to know the indescribable spirit that is love. In the next few lines he adores the beauty of her hair on the pillow and its capture of the moonlight. This is the girl, this is the body of love which is the center of his life. The beloved's softness is seen in the beauty of the sleeping form. In this particular song the author suddenly contrasts the tenderness of the moment with the harsh reality of the young man's life: he has just robbed a store and his punishment lies ahead of him.

Bob Dylan remembers a love of the past in "Girl of the North Country." She is a love who lives far away. The lover of the song remembers her in terms of the need to be protected from the winter, and the beauty of her hair as it falls upon her breast. Does she remember him, this girl of the North Country? In "Hero Blues" Dylan demonstrates he can also be critical of a love which goes against his nature. Love is abused when the beloved wants someone to be a champion for her in the world. If she desires a person who will fight and beat others, she has chosen the wrong man, says Dylan. Such a girl needs a hero out of the history books, not a lover. He reacts with humor to a love which is overly demanding. Dylan is able to convey the tenderness, violence, and comedy of this humanistic love.

This humor is also seen in "All I Really Want to Do." This aspect of love does not demand any change in the beloved's personhood. Such a humanistic love accepts you just the way you are. The lover of Dylan's song does not want to mold his love to his will. In mock seriousness the poet makes plain the uneasy jockeying for interpersonal positions in the love relationship. The humor is good fun, but beneath it ripples a sensuality evoked by the imagery. The lover in the song is saying, "I am teasing and I mean it."

In a like manner he can promise on a very humanistic level that "It Ain't Me, Babe." Dylan is quick to admit that some girls are expecting that which some fellow cannot and perhaps should not provide. He is human in his love. He cannot be a phony hero who will always bear up when the going gets tough.

In many rock love songs there is often a wild quest for love's fruits without commitment. In the Dylan song "Don't Think Twice, It's All Right," the story of such a love is told. The jilted girl is advised that it is no use to call for a love that is gone. The road of the wanderer must be followed. The lover gave his love as he knew it, but she sought his whole being. Noncommitment and pain are elements old in the tradition of the love song. Here Dylan is often true to the folk tradition of humanistic love.

In some of his later songs we find the love tradition expressed in the modern idiom. There is a broadness to the Dylan love song which is raw and tender, yet all the while bordering on the brink of obscurity. In "I Want You" his love for the girl of the song is against reason but still undeniable. All experience and reasoning supports one conclusion concerning this girl: he shouldn't love her. Yet, he cannot lose her. Destiny in some strange way demands that he should want her.

There is a picture of womanhood as beloved in a whole spectrum of trouble, misery, tenderness, and desire in "Just Like a Woman." Dylan is playful and yet moving in this musical picture of the human woman to be loved. She is a woman in all that she does. The way she moves, talks, understands, cries, and suffers touches a strain of femininity rarely touched in an idealized presentation of love.

The often-mentioned humor of Dylan's love material enables him to present the woman with the proper touch of love and human warmth. His "Leopard-Skin Pill-Box Hat" has a touch of

Elaine May and Mike Nichols in their satirical routine on adultery. The English lover in the skit asks to try on his trysting mate's hat.[7] In this obscure Dylan song an animal-skin hat is the main feature of an unfaithful lover. The betrayed man is able to cynically suggest that money and her hat may be the reasons behind her new boyfriend's interest. The new love is expressed in the context of a garage. She left the door to this cheap affair open for all to see.

The love songs of the Beatles feature a very simple lyric line in the early material. In fact, the simplicity and basic "wholesomeness" of the Beatle songs have enabled them to be used by creative teachers in the classroom. One teacher tabulated the words in ten of their most popular songs and found that 173 basic words were used 1,072 times.[8] Most of these words were part of the basic word list for children's reading. By combining the student interest in the Beatles with the task of reading, she was able to increase the motivation of slum children in learning to read.

There is a simple, fresh delight in the teenage ideal of love in most of these early songs. The simplicity of these songs is combined with the early Mersey beat which made the Beatles so famous. Some have seen a dangerous sensuality in the combination of the beat and innocent words. Such a judgment reflects the limited understanding of the beholder.

The student of the meaning and direction of sexual expression at this time has great difficulty in understanding the norms of the age. The *other* generation uses the sharp classifications of an early day when the male fit the stereotype of being a Horatio Alger at work, a John Wayne in the outdoors, and a Stanley Kowalski in love.

A woman, on the other hand, is seen by the *other* generation as a feminine type with characteristic devotion to home-dwelling, baby-tending, husband-worshiping. One could certainly expect to see a clear reflection of these standards in clothing, manners, and heterosexual relationships. What confusion assaults the minds of the *other* generation when they see sexuality expressed in our age! The hair styles, clothing, and casual relationships overwhelm those who still joke about not being able to tell the boys from the girls.

Marshall McLuhan and George B. Leonard have recently indicated that the new age of the global tribe suggests that new directions in the future of sex are being explored now.[9] The *now* generation is discovering the new possibilities for recovering a deeper basis for sexual identity than the superficial marks used in the past. The romantic love of the Middle Ages is being overwhelmed, at last, through the impact of the birth control pill and an awareness of the possibility of interpersonal relationships. Sex, as the final goal to a male and female relationship, is passing away in favor of it being only another of man's many sensitivities. The *now* generation simply doesn't have the hang-up on sex which still possesses the *other* generation. Man is being released from the past to allow real involvement between male and female without the charade of a man having to be strong (never cry!) and a woman helpless (remaining uneducated). The *other* generation's concern with the youth's sexual expression is therefore often quite embarrassing. Those who find rock music erotic and dangerous are speaking of their own reactions and the fear they have for themselves. The rock music often reveals a deepening quest for the content of involvement as persons.

The lyrics of the Lennon songs have undergone a change in the recent past. Perhaps John Lennon has been working on this level all the time. However, it is much clearer to the listener now that a "cool" or interpersonal view of sex is being expressed.

It is true that the simple lyric line undergoes a change in the later Lennon and Harrison material. In "For No One" there seems to be an added concern for the motives and concern behind the love of youth:

> Your day breaks, your mind aches,
> you find that all her words of kindness linger on
> when she no longer needs you.
> And in her eyes you see nothing,
> no sign of love behind the tears—
> cries for no one.
> A love that should have lasted years![10]

In their material for the *Sgt. Pepper's Lonely Hearts Club Band* album, we find a serious commentary on the greatest need in the area of human relationships: loneliness. The song "A Little Help from My Friends" raises questions about the reality of the kind of love praised so often in their earlier records:

> Do you need anybody,
> I need somebody to love.
> Could it be anybody
> I want somebody to love.
> Would you believe in a love at first sight,
> Yes I'm certain that it happens all the time.[11]

The person in the song is not really very sure that the romantic love of the poets will ever happen.

There is another cynical statement of youth's idealistic love in "Getting Better." An angry young man recounts his new adjustment and acceptance of all which was unjust about his life in the past. This loss of critical sensitivity has resulted from his relationship with a girl. It's getting better in a way in which it shouldn't. In "When I'm Sixty-Four" Lennon makes a statement on the fad of romance when it has passed. What will be left? In "All You Need Is Love" Lennon reflects again on the simplicity of the "hot" or past's romantic pursuit of love. The song begins with an orchestra playing the French National Anthem, and then the Beatles slip into a simple lyric line which expresses adoration for "love." Again and again the word is repeated. During this recitation of the word "love," questions are raised about the kind of love one should seek. At the end of the song the endless repetition of the title is matched by the barely audible lyric of an earlier Beatle love song. The last tune buried in the fade-out is "Greensleeves" ("What Child Is This?"). It is tempting to see a theological implication here. Is love as revealed through the Christ Child fading from us as an option, or is it the last resort? Lennon is stating the essence of human existence with others: love.

George Harrison also expresses the new thrust of the Beatle material in "Within You Without You":

> We were talking—about the love that's
> gone so cold and the people,

Who gain the world and lose their soul—
they don't know—they can't see—are
you one of them?
When you've seen beyond yourself—
then you may find, peace of mind, is
waiting there—
And the time will come when you see
we're all one, and life flows on within
you and without you.[12]

It has a quality of the relationship between God and his creation reflected in the Gospel of John (14:17, 20, 27). This philosophical and somewhat mystical statement on human love reveals a long journey from the teenager's first touch of the beloved's hand.

Yet, to the humanistic *now* generation, love cannot be separated from its foundation in man's human form. The flesh and the spirit are now inseparable. The desire to hold the hand of the one loved has become related to the presence of a love which knows a boundlessness of spirit. The young people of our time are on the road to the discovery of freedom from the limited love for the flesh by means of love through the flesh.

2. Interpersonal Relationships: "Venda-Buddy"

We live in an age of speed and crowding. The young married couple sit at their kitchen table in their apartment. Through the wall they hear the distinct voices of the neighboring couple as they argue. "You're so stupid you can't even figure out the grocery bill." "Maybe I'm not the smartest wife, but I'm tired of working every day to put you through school." The husband and wife eating their breakfast feel embarrassed. They are overhearing that which is not meant for their ears. They also know in that moment that the neighbors probably heard them as they fought over a personal matter the night before. When the two husbands find themselves on the elevator together the next day, they don't speak. They have never met. They cannot afford to know each other. The privacy which their surroundings won't permit must be obtained through the process of insulating themselves from interpersonal relationships. Such insulation against human interaction is one of the trials of this age. The young are very concerned with this tension between the need for interpersonal interaction to be human and the need for the freedom of loneliness.

Some theologians have found the important element of theology in our age to be an interpersonal state of being.[13] Man is not seen as the rugged individual who worships God by himself in some closet or comes to public worship for private devotion. He is, rather, one who lives a life under God with and for others. In community one knows the work of the Holy Spirit. One worships to commune with God in the company of the people of God. Man is able to understand and share the substance of the faith as he participates in the life of the church. The dimensions of love, forgiveness, and joy given by God are known as we are fully human with other humans.

With such a theological awareness, one suddenly sees much in the Christian tradition from a very different perspective. Moses was not alone on the mountain top in conversation with God. The Lord told him to get off that pinnacle of loneliness and hear what he is being told as he delivers his people from slavery. Peter, John, and James longed to stay for the mysterious experience of the Transfiguration on the mount with Jesus. The Christ, however, quickly led them back into the realm where people live, suffer, and long for hope. One of the characteristics which marked the early church was the quality of the life together. In the long days which passed after the death and resurrection of Christ, the disciples gathered together. It was a gathered church which witnessed the Holy Spirit moving it into the world. This condition of community included not only moments of mutual joy and assurance, but also an open sharing of confession and forgiveness. There are occasional remnants of this tradition of mutual confession in the New Testament literature (i.e., James 5:16). While this openness and humanistic acceptance of others on the basis of this interpersonal relationship was retained for several centuries and urged by the Reformers, it has passed from the contemporary church.

Research psychologist O. Hobart Mowrer suggests a new group therapy which contains that which was once part of the common life within the church.[14] Honesty about one's past failings must be confessed to a significant other. This is not found in the church of our day. Günter Grass, the German novelist, most tellingly captures the *now* generation's quest for this kind of sharing in places other than the church. Oskar, the fascinating midget drummer in *The Tin Drum*, tells of a night club, the Onion Cellar, which provided such an arena for real sharing. The Onion Cellar reached a large cross section of people. They would gather in a converted basement room with a degree of nervousness. In almost liturgical manner the host would don a shawl and distribute onions to people who:

> . . . wanted to talk, to unburden themselves, but they couldn't seem to get started; despite all their efforts, they left the essential unsaid, talked around it. Yet how eager they were to spill their guts, to talk from their hearts, their bowels, their entrails, to forget about their brains just this once, to lay bare the raw, unvarnished truth, the man within.[15]

The onions granted them the opportunity to cry. In this new freedom the dam of isolation was broken and they were suddenly able to share openly and completely with others. These moments of being fully human with others are very rare inside or outside the church.

The church is in a death struggle to recapture this aspect of its nature. The rock generation is also trying to assert its humanity by seeking meaningful interpersonal relationships while finding the freedom to be a person. Paul Simon voices this longing in his beautiful and haunting song "The Sound of Silence."*

> Hello darkness my old friend,
> I've come to talk with you again,
> Because a vision softly creeping,
> left its seeds while I was sleeping,
> And the vision that was planted in my brain
> still remains within the sound of silence.[16]

The silence of our day is seen as death. Where there isn't an interpersonal sharing there is no life. People try to substitute the reality of this death with noise—but it cannot replace an encounter where people share themselves through words and action. Paul Simon depicts this silent existence as one walking through the dark, cold streets:

> And in the naked light I saw
> ten thousand people maybe more.
> People talking without speaking,
> people hearing without listening
> People writing songs that voices never share
> and no one dare disturb the sound of silence.[17]

There are words, sentences, and verses, but no one is really tuned into another's world. Man is destroying the humanity of another by refusing to accept the other as a person, and thereby man loses his own humanity.

> "Fools!" said I "You do not know
> silence like a cancer grows."
> "Hear my words that I might teach you,
> Take my arms that I might reach you."
> But my words like silent raindrops fell,
> and echoed in the wells of silence.[18]

The young have seen the silence which has grown and cut people from others. They experience the *other* generation not listening to them. The young do not claim the ability to teach others of the meaning of humanity. They simply want to share their needs in order that there may be an exchange between persons. Parents complain to counselors and youth workers that they simply can't understand what the young person is thinking. This cancer grows and grows. Young and old talk at each other but it is usually the sound of silence.

The hospital chaplain entered a patient's room just as the doctor was leaving. The middle-aged man in the bed made a sign of irreverence with his hand to the back of the doctor. The conversation between chaplain and patient was very nice, and the words conveyed friendliness and a sense of being well pleased. However, what was the patient saying non-verbally? Had not the sound of silence been real even with so many words?

The parent is often overwhelmed when talking to a teacher or pastor about his inability to understand what his own son or daughter is trying to say through dress and actions. The tendency to be insensitive to nonverbal communication is expressed humorously in an early scene from the Broadway hit *Luv*. A character is overcome with depression. He finally walks to the highest bridge he can find. He slowly climbs up on the edge in preparation for his leap to death. At that moment a friend comes by and says, "Hi! How are things going?" People express their needs and their gifts of love in many ways. The rock generation is calling for an expansion of interpersonal relationships to be recognized. Behavior patterns or small meaningful acts of the youth are often beyond the interpersonal communicational level of the *other* generation. Do humanity and the quest for a context to be human have to be restricted to known responses, or can there be communication between the subcultures of the day in many informal ways?

The threat of non-existence as a person when separated from meaningful relations is transmitted to the young through the life patterns of the *other* generation. Young people can see the example of the adults with their peripheral relationships. In "The Dangling Conversation"* Simon is again able to carefully and tenderly expose the terror of husband and wife dwelling in the same quarters but not relating significantly:

It's a still life water color,
of a now late afternoon,
As the sun shines through the curtained lace
and shadows wash the room.
And we sit and drink our coffee
we are couched in our indifference,
like shells upon the shore

---

* "The Dangling Conversation" by Paul Simon. © 1966 Charing Cross Music Co. Used with permission of the publisher.

You can hear the ocean roar
in the dangling conversation
and the superficial sighs
the borders of our lives.[19]

The couple sit in the same room and read—she, her Emily Dickinson, and he, Robert Frost. They are caught in the "syncopated time" of non-existence. In the last stanza Simon notes the withdrawal of the relationship to such a degree that even as flesh and bones they don't exist to each other:

Now the room is softly faded
and I only kiss your shadow,
I cannot feel your hand,
you're a stranger now unto me
lost in the dangling conversation
and the superficial sighs
in the borders of our lives.[20]

In the quest for man's humanity at this time, the rock generation speaks boldly about those who *allow* the walls to be built between themselves and the world. In "Hello Goodby" Lennon sets the simple responses which disagree side by side to convey the failure of persons to communicate. One is able to respond affirmatively as the other can only react negatively. Walls made of words separate two people from being with and for each other. What evil of emptiness lies behind the simply stated "Yes" or "No" when out of syncopation (Matt. 5:37).

In "Fixing a Hole," John Lennon provides the picture of a man who has confined his world to protect himself from the uncertainties of interpersonal relationships:

I'm fixing a hole where the rain gets in
And stops my mind from wandering
Where it will go
I'm filling the cracks that ran through
the door
And kept my mind from wandering
Where it will go

And it really doesn't matter if I'm wrong
I'm right
Where I belong I'm right
Where I belong.
See the people standing there who
disagree and never win
And wonder why they don't get in my door.[21]

The practice of blocking the holes in our world to keep our minds from wandering and confronting new ideas and people strongly reminds one of the excellent situation used by Sartre to describe being in relationship to persons. He depicts the event of a person sitting in a park and suddenly discovering the presence of another. It is as if a "drain hole" cuts into your world and siphons away some of your being.[22] In his view, the pain of being a person forces humans to deny the possibility of full existence by having them fill the holes in their world to keep others away. The decision to be lonely is one of the causes of this loss of humanity in our time. Paul Simon states the rationalization and fear which keeps one enclosed in a private world when he writes in "I Am a Rock,"*

I've built walls,
A fortress deep and mighty,
That none may penetrate.
I have no need of friendship;
Friendship causes pain.
It's laughter and it's loving I disdain.
I am a rock,
I am an island.
And a rock can feel no pain;
And an island never cries.[23]

Cold shivers race up and down one's back when the power of this statement is grasped. A man confesses that he is afraid to love and laugh because it also might lead to pain and tears:

---

* "I Am a Rock" by Paul Simon. © 1966 by Charing Cross Music. Used by permission of the publisher.

Don't talk of love;
I've heard the word before;
It's sleeping in my memory
And I won't disturb the slumber
Of feelings that have died.
If I never loved I never would have cried.[24]

The pain, terror, and death of Christ have long been removed from the context of human reality by those who are guardians of the faith. Yet, the members of the *now* generation see in the person of Christ one who knows their pain and their trials. True man is man who is not afraid to cry and to love. John Lennon describes youth's lack of assurance as it faces the future on its own in "Help." The solo person knows he needs another in the process of becoming human:

Help! I need somebody. Help!
Not just anybody. Help!
You know I need someone. Help![25]

In the past he didn't need anybody, but now with time comes more pressure:

I'm not so self assured.
Now I find I've changed my mind,
I've opened up the doors.[26]

This recognition of man's need for others is one of the basic thrusts of the Christian faith and of the *now* generation. Every man cries "help" by some means. Those who can reach out in need to others, live; those who don't, lose their humanity and their lives.

There are those seeking a way out of their loneliness to a meaningful life. They don't know how to escape because there is no one to help. Paul Simon writes about such an isolated man in his "A Most Peculiar Man." A man considered strange by fellow boarders lives within the confines of a self-imposed world. He has only the shelter of a house, a room, and his sealed self. This "peculiar" person earned his reputation by not seeking friends and conversation. He had not extended the kind of self created by the Dale Carnegie techniques for winning acquaintances. The world, therefore, assumed that he was purposefully rejecting it. The song concludes with the bitter fruit of such loneliness by reporting his act of suicide. The people cannot understand such a person. He was not at all like other people.

There is a quality of man refusing to relate to others which makes it an almost aggressive murder. Peter Dean, a young New York artist, graphically captures this element of people feeding on the destruction of others in what he calls "cannibal art." In one canvas he creates a man who has the strange look of the Van Gogh self-portrait. This isolated figure has a mouth bathed in human blood! Peter Dean tells us with his brush, "we eat each other up." This kind of dispassionate delight in the death of a person devoured by the hunger of loneliness and despair is described in John Lennon's "A Day in the Life." A man detached from the morning news has his breakfast with this report:

> I read the news today oh boy
> About a lucky man who made the grade
> And though the news was rather sad
> Well I just had to laugh
> I saw the photograph.
> He blew his mind out in a car
> He didn't notice that the lights had changed
> A crowd of people stood and stared
> They'd seen his face before
> Nobody was really sure
> If he was from the House of Lords.[27]

Youth understands the basic responsibility one person has for others. The smoke and fire of hammering out the new in the context of the old do not blind youth from also seeing their failure to relate significantly to others.

Bob Dylan acknowledges youth's lack of compassion for people with need in his album jacket poem "Some Other Kinds of Songs." He recounts a person's deep emotions as he watches a potential suicide standing on the railing of a bridge. The young person can see a clergyman trying to convince him not to jump. The frightened and desperate man on the edge of death reveals in one glance a terrifying loneliness. The young man on the ground sees this man's despair and must quickly turn to leave. He knows in that moment that deep within himself he wishes that he could watch the man jump to his death! Dylan writes here not of another generation. He speaks of the *now* generation and their struggle for full humanity as they choose or reject other persons. In such moments of critical self-awareness rests the hope of the rock theologian. He can honestly say it the way it is.

Janis Ian also captures the moment of observing another while she prepares to take her life in her song "Insanity Comes Quietly to the Structured Mind." It is a moving description of cold systems leading a lonely person to death. The girl who watches in the song must cut off her emotion and control her humanity:

> . . . I turn my head and made my bed
> nothing really need be said cause she is dead.[28]

A bitter comment about society and a critical commentary on some of the young who allow structures to overwhelm their humanity.

Chicago's Second City Players express man's need for others in a depersonalized world in their popular skit "Venda-Buddy." A lonely man on the "El" platform finds himself confronted by a machine which promises to be his buddy for small change. He laughs at such an idea until he is finally hooked by a need to talk to someone or even some thing. He will even feed it coins to find another who cares. Using the same concept, Paul Simon describes loneliness and its frustration with life in "The Big Bright Green Pleasure Machine." In this satire of what might be called a singing commercial for escapism, the characteristics of the loser are depicted. The poor soul who is the butt of everyone else's humor or hostility is always out of step with

the successful person. He is the kind of person who can't wear
tennis shoes when they are "in" with the hip crowd because
he has arch problems. Some guys win the girl. He doesn't. The
ultimate loser needs a big bright green pleasure machine.

How do the strange and lonely reach out to human flesh
in this humanistic age? The young person feels the pressure to
be accepted because he knows intuitively that he must find
others, and he is ready too often to give anything to meet this
need. This attempt to find others is a significant quest theo-
logically for humanity with other people. The tragedy of man's
isolation and destruction is much in the thinking of the *now*
generation. There is an isolation from others which surrounds
those who are leading battles in the unstructured thrust for
human justice. Out in front of the changing troops and varying
opponents, good men and women have become victims of para-
noia due to the loneliness of leadership and struggle.

On the other hand, our literature does affirm the possibility
of friends, present or past. In Bob Dylan's song of friendship
long lost, we find a deep importance given to one finding his
humanity in the context of other people. He can write in
"Bob Dylan's Dream" about the emotional hangover one has
when friends are no longer around. The lazy memories of
shared troubles, happy songs and stories, make the mind ache
for that which cannot return. In these lines Dylan says that
friends have made his humanity of the past real, and the memories linger on. Contemporary interpersonal relationships can
also be the supportive element to existence, as John Lennon
writes in "With a Little Help from My Friends":

> What do I do when my love is away.
> (Does it worry you to be alone)
> How do I feel by the end of the day
> (Are you sad because you're on your own)
> No I get by with a little help from my
> friends[29]

The need for the other can also make a person feel the rejection
of a friend even more deeply. Bob Dylan cynically comments

on fair-weather friendship in "Positively 4th Street." He learns
of this kind of relationship when things run against him. When
he is down and beaten, such "friends" smile and get pleasure
from seeing the turn of bad luck hit him. It is the wish of
everyone in such a situation to have the roles changed. If the
so-called friend could just understand for a moment how the
betrayed one looks at such an expression of false friendship,
he would know rejection. The spectrum of man fighting isolation
in the quest for humanity is very much a part of the *now* generation's scene. The rock writer's assertion of man's need for others
is also very much within the Christian tradition, as Bonhoeffer
expressed it, being "a man for others."[30]

3. Zest for Life: "The Live-In"

The subculture under study is humanistic in its approach to
life. There is a zest for life which is fast, gentle, and a bit
out of sorts with some of the past conceptions. Superficially,
at least, America compels every person to face a kind of living
which includes cars, lawns, do-it-yourself basement shops, and
lots of television. Man's use of the new leisure society has not
yet been fully established. The thrust of the shorter work
schedules and increased free time raises a major question of
the nature of humanity in the freedom of leisure. The younger
generation isn't turned on by the prospect of watching television every evening. Perhaps this is just the nature of an age
difference. There is, however, an affirmation of life on the
humanistic level which may suggest new areas of thought.

In Paul Simon's "The 59th Street Bridge Song" we find the
kind of happiness and joy which might puzzle some of the
other generation. Calmly and happily the song describes a day
with no work to do and no commitment to anyone or anything.
The last line carries the affirmation that life is joyous and to be
loved. This is not a humanity caught in the swirl of activity
and work. One just kicks tin cans and smells flowers. In John
Lennon's lyric for "Good Day Sunshine" the love theme is
expressed in a similar awareness of nature:

Good day sunshine,
Good day sunshine,
Good day sunshine.
I need to laugh and when the sun is out
I've got something I can blab about.
I feel good in a special way,
I'm in love and it's a sunny day.[31]

In our discussion of rebellion and the youth's reaction to the work ethic, there will be an attempt to understand some of the forces which produce this dynamic change as has been manifested in the hippy crowd. It is possible to note here that the new humanistic concern of this generation changes a number of basic views now maintained by much of the *other* generation. The sacred belief that human meaning can only be discovered in relation to a job and its rewards in terms of material possessions is passing. There is a humanistic rediscovery of the created order. The whole "in" movement (love-ins, be-ins, sit-ins, etc.) indicates that the subculture is saying something to the older generation. Young people are not protesting against things, but rather seeking to be *in* them. The papers and popular magazines are now filled with the doings of the hippy crowd. This small group of individuals is seeking a simple, uncomplicated existence where a person can express himself through love, vision, and freedom.

Drugs and their role in turning on the generation will be discussed later. However, the effect of the hippy rediscovery of the religiously simple life reaches deeply into the lives and philosophy of the *now* generation. As policemen carry away hippies from a mass love-in, they are met not with cries of dismay and anger. The young girl just says to the policemen as they carry her to the police van, "I love you, I love you."

Some have said that such a quest to be a new person which must deny society is a new sort of monastic existence. This is not quite true. The love of humanity is so much a part of this rejection of the superficial that others are touched by the power of this movement's integrity. John Lennon's word pictures in "Lucy in the Sky with Diamonds" give one a fantasy view of life while retaining a certain reality as a basis:

> Picture yourself in a boat on a river,
> With tangerine trees and marmalade skies
> Somebody calls you, you answer quite slowly,
> A girl with kaleidoscope eyes.
> Cellophane flowers of yellow and green,
> Towering over your head.[32]

The language is obscure and tainted like the world seen through kaleidoscope sunglasses. Love and the idealized woman are in the sky and yet perhaps very close:

> Picture yourself on a train in a station,
> With plasticine porters with looking glass ties,
> Suddenly someone is there at the turnstile,
> The girl with the kaleidoscope eyes.[33]

George Harrison, the Beatle interested in the music and instruments of India, writes about this world with its zest for meaningful existence in "Within You Without You":

> We were talking—about the space
> between us all
> And the people—who hide themselves
> behind a wall of illusion
> Never glimpse the truth—then it's far
> too late—when they pass away.
> . . . . . .
> We were talking—about the love that's
> gone so cold and the people,
> Who gain the world and lose their soul—
> they don't know—they can't see—are
> you one of them?[34]

This is the lingering question of man and his relationship to life. This is more than an invitation to "drop out." If one can only recover his humanity by leaving the rat-race, then he must.

However, there is here the possibility of living with a freedom in the world.

Such possibilities are disturbing to young and old. For example, the college graduate in the executive training program can only give such thinking a fleeting glance. How can he seek such a zest for life? One such young man had been in the training program for six months. He had just moved into one of the business offices. He was told to check the procedure of the department and report anything which seemed outdated and out of order. The young executive in training quickly realized that the two older men in the office were fearful of his presence and viewed the report he might make as a real threat to their jobs. When the newcomer reported the discomfort he felt in doing such a job, he was sent to the company's psychologist. After several sessions with the psychologist the young man said that he could now accept what he had previously considered to be unethical.

Can one be free to enjoy life as a human within such conforming structures? Every man must struggle to answer that as best he can. This is one of the deep concerns of the *now* generation being expressed in the rock music: man must choose a meaningful existence which can enable him to enjoy the created order and other people. We will look at aspects of this major thrust in our discussion of rebellion on behalf of others.

The Experiential Generation: "Unless I See . . . Place My Finger . . . and Place My Hand . . ." (John 20:25)

1. Experience Everywhere: "Please Touch!"

The group of fifteen well-dressed people looked quite uncomfortable as they were seated in a small circle of folding chairs that had been placed in the parking lot of the busy supermarket. They sat in the midst of their curious suburban neighbors as part of a study group from their church. They had planned to study the book of Acts in the shelter of a church basement. The men and women were nervous, embarrassed, and confused by this change of location. The pastor began the study of Paul's difficulty with the crowds in the market place. The people were hostile and resentful. However, the study was undertaken in that place in order that the people might encounter the thrust of the biblical message with their minds and their *experience*.

It can't be underlined too often that one of the important attributes of the media orientation of our day is experience. Television puts the viewer in the midst of the joys and sufferings of the peoples of the world. He experiences with others that which was alien to him in the past. The church's teaching in some places is beginning to reflect this fact.

As the Apostle Thomas wanted to experience with his eyes, fingers, and hands that the Christ had indeed risen, so the early church recognized the importance of experience. With the death of the generation which experienced Jesus as a companion and teacher, it became essential to worry about those "who have not seen and yet believe" (John 20:29b).

Liturgy, among other things, has at its best been a recital of God's promise and presence in such a way that the people of God experience this content.

The *now* generation is tuned into an experience of existence which finds delight in the unexpected, unusual, and the fresh. The "happening" is an artistic response to this need. Not long ago a group of people gathered in a small storefront building on the south side of Chicago. The participants paid their $1.50 and took their seats which encircled the room. A cast of several people led two hours of action art which unfolded in the midst of all those present. A sink in the corner became Lake Michigan. A baby buggy was pushed back and forth. The happening was concluded as gunny sacks fell from the ceiling onto the heads of the audience. This final act represented, in the artist's eyes, feces dumped on the audience. This is action, happening, and participation. It is really unplanned and different on each occasion.

The senses, as an extension of man, have long been recognized as the means by which man enjoys art. The development of the senses in the appreciation of beauty is what enables the beholder to be grasped by that which is both without and within himself. Even the sharp senses of physical need can be a means to aid the experience of life. Ernest Hemingway, in *A Moveable Feast*, comments on the aesthetic quality of hunger:

> There you could always go into the Luxembourg museum and all the paintings were sharpened and clearer and more beautiful if you were belly-empty, hollow-hungry. I learned to understand Cézanne much better and to see truly how he made landscapes when I was hungry.[1]

The senses of youth are sharpened by the media orientation of the day. Young people hunger to experience life and its meanings with all of their being. As the legendary safecracker files his nails to make his fingertips sensitive to the safe tumblers, so has this generation been prepared sensually to respond to the fine movements and demands of life.

The rock music of our time cannot be separated from the experiential and spontaneous aspects of the *now* generation. The music idiom is the literature and poetry of the youth's world. It is not written and published for hardback books. It is happening on records and is not created to endure, but just to be now. Dylan writes poetry on the jackets of the albums. This is literature which involves the listener as participant. When the Beatles were searching for a studio to give them a chance at making a record, one production man rejected them because he was convinced that electric guitars were finished as a popular instrument. It is, of course, easy now to know how wrong he was. In fact, the increased electrification of nearly every instrument indicates an important part of the sub-culture's need for experience. The tuned-up amplifiers become an extension of the artist's nervous system as performer and listener are welded into one. The musicians "plug into" the electronic mixer which enables music and lyrics to become one. Bob Dylan was booed at the Newport Folk Festival for his "rock" interest. However, even the dean of folk singers, Pete Seeger, has joined the folk-rock bards by using electric backing.

One of the delightful things about the "coffee house craze" which is sweeping the country, is its marvelous spontaneity. Each person relates to others and is free to allow anything to happen. There are now over 2,000 such informal forums for conversation and creative expression. Every night at a coffee house is different from the last as people experience the un-expected in conversation and viewpoints.

The *now* generation reflects this new orientation toward experience and spontaneity particularly in its group activities. Those working with young people today find little success in reaching them when they adhere to the concepts of another generation which needed to belong to organizations. The *now* generation does not want to join organizations and be committed for long periods of time. Bob Dylan spoke for many when he recently remarked, "I can't make it with any organization!"[2]

The youth of today want to be where the action is. These generalizations have far-reaching implications for those trying to work with students on the campus, in local churches, or in the neighborhood. It places a demanding burden on those who work with youth to make content and media meaningful and consistent with where the generation is.

The educational orientation of our time encourages one to explore and challenge what has been accepted solely on authority from the past. Bob Dylan has captured the spirit of spontaneous experience in "Mr. Tambourine Man." The sound of the tambourine seems to reflect the sparkling glitter of a lazy morning. The captivated person of the song is not really tired or lazy. He just wants to drink deeply of the freedom and joy of being alive. He is ready to follow this piper of free experience on any road with his weary senses. The wanderer is prepared to chase a shadow in search of a refreshing experience. He concludes with a plea for an experience which will overwhelm the realities of today which often sap human energy and goodness. Let the darkness and pain of human existence be bathed in the stunning ring of the tambourine man. Maybe tomorrow today's starkness can be endured.

Arlo Guthrie reflects this same mad desire to experience the unexpected and unstructured aspects of life in his song "Ring Around-a-Rosy Rag." A friend is jailed for suddenly dancing in the park late at night. The disorderly exercise in noise and madness is completely without meaning:

> ring around, ring around-a-rose
> touch your nose and blow your toes and mine
> doing the ring around-the-rosy rag[3]

Such a happening is fun. The spirit is unleashed and refreshed by the childlike game. Part of the fun comes from the scandalized adults who cannot understand this zeal for experience.

This desire to leave the rut and strike out for the next experience is a theme captured again, humorously, in Dylan's "Outlaw Blues." The rebel against society wishes that he could strike out into a new country. Australia is often chosen as a new

home by those who are dissatisfied with America. Adult pro-
testors against expressions of big government often journey to
the land down-under to start a new life of individual freedom.
The boy in the song seeks this faraway place because he wants
the experience of change.

The love of the unexpected and unusual is found in Dylan's
"She Belongs to Me." A girl is depicted as being a fountain of
jewelry and light. She glitters like a gem. She is strange and
believes in the science of clouding men's minds. What an experience! This love for the unusual is evoked in the wild and
colorful clothing and wearing apparel that have now conquered
the youth scene.

The emphasis on experience also presents the awareness that
the direction of it all is not clear. Paul Simon expresses, in
"Cloudy," a sense of unanswered inquiry which is both the
nature of life and the state of his mind. The sky is filled with
clouds which are a mixture of colors. There is an uncertainty
about their place of origin or where they are going. It is hard to
know whether they offer a forecast of hope or despair. Like
a giant inkblot test the sky reflects the questions about life's
meaning in the beholder's eyes. Experience, viewed as fate, is
beautifully set forth in "Patterns." Leaves, rustling in the night,
cast patterns upon the wall of a lonely person's room. The
patterns of one's life are woven across the spectrum of human
life. They are there in the instant of new life and remain until
the moment of physical death. Simon utilizes the realism of
physical life to find unchanging patterns to existence. The passage of time with its payment in age like the hue of one's skin
cannot be altered. Here is a pessimism similar to that expressed
in the book of Ecclesiastes. There is that basic resignation about
the direction of experience: "For everything there is a season,
and a time for every matter under heaven" (3:1). Yet, one must
learn the range of his experience by living.

2. *The Search for Experience*

Such a view is not at all new. At almost any job interview,
great stress is placed on recording the young person's previous

experience. Parents resort to the age-old argument as long as they are able to get away with it—when trying to convince youth of the value of the parents' decision: "When you are as old as we are and have experienced as much as we have . . . " How does one get experience of life's wholeness without being destroyed by it? The *now* generation is turned on by contemporary culture, its tradition from the past, its educational goals, its advertising, and even its historical religion. Yet, the fear of the *other* generation by the young is real and understandable. The youth of today must seek their own depression or other economic and social crisis, which they have been told by the *other* generation was a golden age of one finding oneself. The youth do not have the opportunity to experience life and their relationship to it through their usefulness to a home industry of the past where they would be needed to keep the family economic unit alive.

Several hundred thousand young people run away from home each year. They may try to join a hippy community. However, this isn't possible for most. Bob Dylan was able to find his own economic depression of suffering and discover experience as a runaway. For others, the Army is a way of experiencing life with the spontaneity removed.

College has opened a means of coming to life with its many experiences. The good college opportunity throws the student into a lion's den of conflicting viewpoints and options about life. Numerous life styles and perspectives about everything are manifested in this world of the campus. Spontaneity is plentiful and totally absorbing. There is often a strong attempt on the part of college administrations and parents to insulate the student from such an opportunity.

This parental reluctance to have the student personally experience life is best understood against a background of what can happen. There are three areas which most concern the *other* generation as the *now* generation undertakes the quest to experience life: drugs, language, and sex.

3. *The Drug Bag as Experience*

The drunken party, with everyone "losing control" of himself, has been vividly etched into the minds of the general public either from personal experience or from the entertainment media. At this time in the experience of young people it is probably more fitting to talk about drugs. They are "in" because they help one get a "high" to be "tuned in." The current music does not talk about drinking. However, it does carry the strong influence of drug or mind-expanding experience. The hippy community, with a life of love outside the rat race of society, attributes the big musical breakthrough to the Beatles with their electric sound and their basic freedom from the "uptight" society.

We now have musical groups which claim a "psychedelic" sound. Paul McCartney, the music-writing Beatle, is reported to have admitted several LSD trips in the recent past. The Beatles and other music personalities have publicly supported the legalization of marijuana in England. The Beatles became the disciples of a Hindu guru or teacher. They later deserted this teacher, but have maintained a deep interest in meditation. The disciple of meditation has led them to reject the whole drug scene. If they had known about the inner creative strength which could be unleashed by spiritual insight, they claim that they would have never tried drugs. There is a strong anti-drug movement in some of the East coast music.

The drug picture in our time is much different than the old charges that jazz musicians were "on dope." The drugs which appeal in our day enable a person to have an experience in which the mind and senses explode into another realm of existence. These mind-expanding drugs are not habit-forming and are usually taken in community with others. It is feared by some medical authorities that there are side effects which are quite dangerous.

It is unfortunate that a portion of our society is forced to escape from growing up through the use of drugs. It is even more unfortunate that the world should be in such a state that it is not a place which would encourage the young to want to mature in it.

A drug ethic is needed in our day which can be applied to a complex problem. The nature of this problem is well illustrated in a dramatic radio advertisement which appeared on many stations. A young man is being praised for having closed a very difficult sale. The manager says, "I don't know what has happened to you these past few weeks, but you seem much more relaxed. Now you have confidence and are able to close those sales. I think that you are ready for the big promotion. I am making you regional sales manager!" The young man is overwhelmed by the sudden turn of events. He is quick to add, however, that the credit must be given to a drug he can now buy at the store without prescription. This is the key to his success. This is not a portion of Aldous Huxley's *Brave New World*. The advertising campaign, with its assorted examples of one's need for the drug, is being beamed across the country. Success in a bottle!

In our day many doctors see patients and quickly prescribe tranquilizing drugs when nervousness is reported. Some patients claim that physicians simply ask them to decide whether they want such a drug or not. What is the ethical position for the high school district that has a large bowl of tranquilizing drugs in the administrative lounge? The harried school officials simply drop a dime in a cup and take them whenever they need them in the day. How does one decide what is abuse and what is acceptable in the use of drugs?

Ignatius, the early church father, wrote to the Ephesians during the early part of the second century that they should stay close to the experience of the sacrament. The bread is "the medicine of immortality, the antidote for death."[4] To some, the power of the Lord's Supper can be described with medical or pharmaceutical terminology because it offers assurance, freedom, and community outside the experience of daily existence. Must one under no condition touch any drug at all? As one listens to the *now* generation talking about the rationale behind their use of drugs, it does not remain very clear how we can judge between the hopped-up salesman and the young person seeking communion of experience with a god outside himself through the use of drugs. The church must address its gospel to the use of drugs in our whole society. The past theological inclination to cast a blanket condemnation on all uses of drugs does not remain consistent with the Good News which meets people where they are and understands what they are saying about their need.

Most young people do not directly experience life through drugs. However, the music of our time does have an experiential dimension which digs deeply into the heart, mind, and senses of youth. A difference in tuning explains the difficulty of the *other* generation to tolerate the sound of rock music. The older listener does not feel his body and mind moving with it. As we have previously noted, the difference in orientation and communication often results in a value judgment without understanding what is really going on.

The so-called psychedelic music is basically rock music with added electrification, and abstraction of lyric. The terms "trip" or "happening" may appear in the verse. However, the drug interest must be seen as merely part of the great influence of experience and spontaneity in a society discovering its senses anew. The drug interest is the result of the age's sensitivity and not the cause of this quest for experience.

In the later works of Dylan and the Beatles, lyric and sound are used as an added attempt to experience through experimentation. In "Visions of Johanna" Dylan shares the spontaneous visions of the night. Words of the song seem to run over one another in a stream of consciousness style. The use of a proper name brings word associations which demonstrate an experience and joy in language as an extension of feelings. The same love for experience through the language of random experience is seen in "Stuck Inside of Mobile with the."

The Beatles' growth and development have surprised and even displeased some fans. The simple lyric of the Mersey beat days is gone. They now sample deeply in the music of India and the unlimited possibilities of electronic experimentation. It seems as if the Beatles are leading the way into the future of this age of experience. Their later long-playing albums vividly show us the distance they have come from the early discs. *Rubber Soul, Revolver, Sgt. Pepper's Lonely Hearts Club Band,* and *Magical Mystery Tour* also indicate a growing introspection.

It is clear in the *Sgt. Pepper's Lonely Hearts Club Band* album that the statement(s) on loneliness has been made through the whole album. It is a totality and not just a collection of unrelated songs. The album opens with the familiar or at least traditional setting of a party band. This gathering of people with its brass music is quickly dissolved into the individualistic loneliness of persons experiencing the pain and trials of life.

The language of the mind-expanding experience is seen in "Lucy in the Sky with Diamonds":

> Picture yourself in a boat on a river,
> With tangerine trees and marmalade skies
> Somebody calls you, you answer quite slowly,
> A girl with kaleidoscope eyes.
> Cellophane flowers of yellow and green,
> Towering over your head.
> Look for the girl with the sun in her eyes,
> And she's gone.[5]

The colors explode and overwhelm the senses. The facets of a diamond flood the vision as one identifies with the language of the song. The song paints a world of color and idealization. This is not a song about LSD dreams. Yet, it captures the very heart of experience in freedom.

The Beatle sound in *Sgt. Pepper's Lonely Hearts Club Band* is unbelievable. The Beatles create with their music what is an experience of the emotions and senses to the listener. In spending four intense months of work on this album, the Beatles reflect an introspective rock music which enables the listener to spontaneously allow feelings to be part of the musical experience. The Grateful Dead, the Jefferson Airplane, and the Doors are examples of the rock composers/musicians who are particularly close to the hippy image. However, they represent one of the many quests for experience which is part of the whole rock scene.

4. *Language as Experience*

An understanding of the use of language in the rock music world is important if one cares to know what is happening. The young have been looked upon as having a language world of their own. Parents at different points of intersection with this form of verbal communication have reacted with dismay and despair. They accuse the users of this subcultural idiom of speaking slang or non-English. The role of language has always been important. Some students of English usage reject the traditional objective norms for correctly spoken English. They view the development and use of language as being something quite fluid and in continuous flux. People who support such an outlook contend that proper language is determined by popular usage.

Subcultures within a society find meaning and cohesion as groups through the binding quality of special word usage and dialect. Common laborers, scholars in the same field, and even salesmen have their own vocabulary. The group of people following the Christ developed a form of communication others could not readily understand. Jesus spoke in the dialect of the hills which seemed strange to those of the city. The choice of words and their special meanings often confused his listeners (i.e., "wind" and "spirit" in John 3:1 ff.). As the church has incorporated more followers from diverse cultural backgrounds, it has had to struggle with the endless tension between traditional terminology and new word choices. The problem of relating faith and language in a meaningful way has not been resolved by the church in our day.

One can quickly determine the progress of a youth worker's relationship to his charges by the flow of mutual vocabulary. The sensitive youth worker finds himself not only sharing the language of the young people, but he also discovers that his vocabulary is being used by them. This has probably been one of the most telling indicators of the popularity and influence of the rock music scene on the *now* generation. The Beatles did not try to copy the language of their following. They boldly introduced a whole new idiom that the youth scene absorbed from them! The world was quickly buzzing with terms such as "fab," "gear," and "kinky."

The beautiful and meaningful lyric material of the Beatles, Paul Simon, Janis Ian, Bob Dylan, and others is filled with the subculture's idiom of today. Paul Simon, for example, uses the contemporary language of the rock world in his "Blessed" with striking effect. He does not use the *other* generation's terms for addicts and nice-looking women, but rather the latest hip terms for these blessed people of the youth subculture.

Dylan "blows minds" and fills his songs with references and images which are sometimes beyond the comprehension of both the *other* and *now* generations. Youth is able to experience the thrust of the rock material because its language hits them where they live, think, and feel. The Christian is forced to reflect both on the judgment of old, when people were scattered and spoke many tongues (Tower of Babel), and on the responsibility given on the day of Pentecost when the people of many tongues became one in understanding through the witness of the church. Where does the community of God stand today when the world does not understand its language and its experience, and when the church is not even sure of its own understanding? Can the church start listening before it talks? To what does it listen? How does it listen?

5. *Sex as Experience*

The other aspect of youthful experience which worries the older generation is sex. Our age is aware of the fact that sex encompasses a vast terrain of human life. The *other* generation is fearful for the *now* generation as it awakens to homo-, hetero-, and solitary sexual expression. However, one is amazed how few young people really have a hangup on sex. On the one hand, the parent is scandalized by the scene in the foreign film which shows two nude girls wrestling with the young photographer. On the other hand, the young people spend three hours discussing the film and do not mention that scene at all!

The call for free sexual expression is within, around about, and before every young person. A theologian has recently talked about sex in terms of "good sex" as being distinguishable from that which the advertisers use to peddle everything.[6] The church has been neglecting its responsibility concerning the expression of sex in human life. It has failed to articulate its view of sex and sexual freedom while relinquishing the hour to *Playboy*, which has taken a serious interest in theology. The editors are able to get distinguished theologians to write articles intelligible to others than specialists. The goodness of man's body and life has often been buried in the fears and distorted views of the past. The fresh and honest biblical awareness of man's joy in loving a person by giving himself completely to another has been lost.

The advent of reliable means of contraception, the car as a dating vehicle, the available medical cure for venereal disease, and the chance to understand what is happening on the level of a physical relationship have changed the *now* generation's view of past mores. The reassessment of the person as male and female in clothing and behavior by the *now* generation has resulted in a new "cool" view of sexuality. The meaning of persons tends to place sex as only one of man's many senses. The songs of the rock generation are not particularly "sexy."

There is the realm of experience which does include the appreciation and exploration of the human body. Some have seen strong (and evil) sexuality being expressed in the modes of dancing and even the beat which drives on the rock music. To judge, for example, that the Beatle song "I Wanna Hold Your Hand" is latent with sexuality because of the ecstatic musical intensity on the word "hand," is to read into the material something that only the beholder can see. The dancing of our time is a great release of energy and makes one expressively satisfied. However, contemporary dancing, a group charade done to music, cannot be judged as having more sexual overtones than dancing of any period—from ancient biblical tribal dances to the present.

We have seen in our discussion of love that there are references to the human body and even the satisfaction of seeing

your beloved asleep at night beside you in bed. Some of the
early Beatle numbers reflect the physical enjoyment of this
generation in touching, holding, and being near the girl or guy
loved. This recognition of "love's body" may be the best thing
to happen to a Christian. Such an acknowledgment summons
him to live wholly committed to Christ through his sensual and
emotional awareness to the body of life. There is a humanistic
basis to sexual expression which seeks a meaningful relationship
between persons as the foundation of a love association.

The experience of knowing the reality of the Incarnation in
Jesus Christ was important to those "who had seen." During
the days immediately following the resurrection, such firsthand
experiences of the risen Lord enabled a rebirth of broken men.
Jesus would not deny Thomas the chance to satisfy his doubts
with the experience of touching and feeling even the marks of
suffering and death upon the body of God's love (John 20:19-
29). The *now* generation pleads for a life in which man may
know the reality of hope, love, and suffering through the touch
and experience of others. Such an experiential existence cannot
be denied the young, even by those who have ceased to experience life and faith.

The Anti-Work Generation:
"What Do You Want to Do?" "Nothing!"

The employment manager looks up at the tall man standing in front of his desk. "Are you hiring?" The manager's eyes scan the empty employment application which the man could not fill out because he could not write. "What can you do?" The poorly dressed man stares at the company official for a few moments. "I can do anything a mule can do."

The American's dream of education for everyone makes us want to believe that such extreme cases will soon vanish from our society. The Protestant work ethic forces us to believe that God calls us to our place of work and that our worth as human beings stems from our faithful performance in that job— no matter how unimportant or poorly paying it might be. Another unexamined American maxim affirms that any person using imagination, interior drive, and hard work can reach the heights of success with God's blessing. We are participating in a time when these self-evident truths are breaking down.

Man is finding it more and more difficult to discover his identity in relation to his job. In the words of a character in Ralph Ellison's novel *Invisible Man*, "They got all this machinery, but that ain't everything; *we the machines inside the machine.*"[1] How does man remain man without becoming a machine himself in this day of rapid technological change? The old Puritan ethic of work still gives some people an uneasy feeling about the non-labor jobs prevalent in our society. There isn't the good

old muscular exchange between man and his work which once
seemed to seal the validity of the worker's right to receive his
food and lodging. Levin, in Tolstoy's novel *Anna Karenina*,
finds this mystical satisfaction as he joins his workers in cutting
hay with a hand scythe:

> In the very heat of the day the mowing did not seem such hard
> work to him. The perspiration with which he was drenched
> cooled him, while the sun, that burned his back, his head, and his
> arms, bare to the elbow, gave vigor and increased his persever-
> ance to his labor; and more and more often now came those
> moments of unconsciousness, when it was possible not to think
> of what one was doing. The scythe cuts of itself. These were
> happy moments. Still more delightful were the moments when
> they reached the stream where the rows ended, and the old
> man . . . rinsed its [the scythe's] blade in the fresh water of the
> stream, ladled out a little in a tiny dipper, and offered Levin
> a drink.[2]

Such work jobs are rapidly being eliminated from industry.
Our society is not prepared for the fact that there are those who
will not be able to change to meet the more skilled tasks and
who must remain unemployed. Are such people, who can no
longer be employed, hearing a gospel which can shake off the
old Puritan ethic and assume a new understanding of man's
calling and purpose apart from the job context?

Another aspect of the work problem confronting contemporary youth as it views a future occupation is the frequent necessity to participate in work which serves a dishonest end. Paul
Goodman attributes this condition to the whole consumer- and
business-oriented economy which results in jobs of questionable
integrity.[3] The young know the meaninglessness of being a
craftsman who must restore an automobile tailfin when it has
been designed to become obsolete next year, to be costly to
repair, and to be dangerous. What sense of satisfaction can the
automotive body repairman have as a part of this conspiracy?

The salesman also often feels a struggle with his conscience
as he works hard at his job. In the words of Lenny Bruce, "The
term itself, 'selling,' implies talking the customer into purchasing
an article he has not previously had any need or desire for."[4]

There are salesmen who do not change minds or force things upon people. They are probably more accurately called clerks. For the young, the idea of pressuring others to do that which they had not planned to do is a bit distasteful. How can anyone find honest meaning in his work when there is an underlying question of its morality? A survey of 800 college seniors reveals that the lure of money no longer determines the young person's orientation toward work. Henry C. Wallich comments that "money clearly is losing ground, both as a means to creature comforts and as a status symbol . . . people long ago stopped finding it attractive to be fat once almost everybody could afford to overeat."[5]

Dietrich Bonhoeffer has reminded us that the true Christian ethic at this point is one which sees the Christian as a man committed first to Christ and *then* made free to serve Christ at his place in the world. This is not the act of blessing that which is the dehumanizing or dishonest in the labor world. In Christ,

> . . . a man takes up his position against the world *in* the world; the calling is the place at which the call of Christ is answered, the place at which a man lives responsibly.[6]

It is implicit in such a theological position that man is not necessarily limited to a job or work as a means of discovering his opportunity to respond to Christ.

Perhaps the future holds a workless society or a world where the leisure life is the major part of man's time. The use of leisure time as meaningful time is most difficult for modern man. Many of those who have already won the short work week of the future get other jobs on the side to keep busy. Can man find his humanity in the play, sport, and pleasure of the leisure society of the near future? A parable of this dilemma peculiar to modern times is enacted each year at McAlester, Oklahoma. The penitentiary there holds a rodeo which draws 26,000 fans. The big event is a battle between a band of men serving life sentences and seven bulls. Each bull has a pair of tobacco sacks tied to its horns. One of the sacks contains a cash prize of $50.

The men risk their lives in this forced leisure to face the bulls and the reward.[7] What is the meaning to life revealed in such a use of time? What manner of men are these who watch and who wrestle the bulls?

The whole society is about to face the reality of life with time on its hands. Youth cannot seriously entertain a work ethic which has been altered by this fact of the present times. They must seek new answers in a world of leisure. Leisure is no longer a mere interlude between two work periods. It may become the root of man's humanity. Changing in minor respects the axiom about children, we might predict, "play will be the work of *man*." How frustrating it is for the older person to see the young living with enjoyment in leisure. As forerunners for the workless society, they appear as lazy and worthless to those nursed on sweat, competition, and financial ambition. Arlo Guthrie appears to some as a stalking-horse for tomorrow's worthless society when he can sing in "The Motorcycle Song":

> I don't want a pickle
> just want to ride on my motorsickle
> And I don't want a tickle
> cause I'd rather ride on my motorsickle
> And I don't want to die
> just want to ride on my motorscy[8]

Play and fun are here to be enjoyed by the future adult.

It is clear that we are living in a time when the young do not accept the old work ethic. They see no mystical good in work itself. The *now* generation would rather dutifully consume and in that way keep the economy going as all advertising and even presidential statements urge. The frontier, farm-oriented understanding of work has passed. It lingers only in the consciences of the *other* generation.

It is understandable that the rock music of our day should reflect this change in work attitudes. Bob Dylan captures the sad state of man's lot as he is caught between the revolution of the future and the despair of today in his "Ballad of Hollis Brown." A poor man, living outside of town with his five children and wife, searched for work so he could provide for his family. The food is gone and the well is dry. He is a man losing his humanity because there is no support and no work. Why has this happened? Why can't I be a man and be allowed to earn my way? He prays to God for a friend and no one comes. The broken shell of a man takes his last dollar and purchases seven shells for his shotgun. Seven shots ring out and seven bodies rest on the floor of a poor man's farmhouse. However, the break between the past and present mind-sets is not resolved. In another poverty setting seven more humans are born to be without work.

Man and his quest for the fulfillment of his job to make a living and be a man are vividly depicted in Dylan's "Who Killed Davey Moore?" The tragedy of a sick, aged boxer fighting to earn a small amount for his wife and children is frozen into a series of verses which record each portion of society trying to clear itself of responsibility in his death. Nobody will claim responsibility for this man's deathly work. Each sector of the participants in this sport knew the stakes and the desperate nature of Davey Moore's physical condition. To society this labor of destruction seemed right.

It isn't just the poor being captured by necessity in their struggle for a job. Paul Simon beautifully relates the story of the poor who watch and wish to be successful in "Richard Cory." After relating the enormous wealth and position of the man for whom the poor man works, he writes that the workers admired the philanthropic character of this great man. He had the ability to drink with the boys and remember their small needs. The little man quivers with appreciation for his many displays of concern. The average man in quest of survival was overwhelmed by the newspaper banner which proclaimed that this captain of industry sent a well-placed piece of lead through his temple. Simon responds with the chorus of every man's goal by expressing the worker's wish that he were Richard Cory. My daily labor, my unpaid bills, my desire for more of everything, compel me to be wealthy at any cost, at any danger to myself.

The rich and the poor are trapped by their desire to get out of the pit of poverty at any cost. The poor worker is willing to trade the inhumanity of his machine for the meaninglessness of position and wealth. Man, rich or poor, secretly knows the deadly cost he must pay to walk the treadmill of work and success for the sake of production. The young do not want to enlist in such a line of marchers passing through the corporate structure of a consumer society.

The rock generation is often tempted to point the finger at the Richard Corys who promote the hopeless arms race. In "Masters of War" Dylan singles out those in power who have used work to bring literal destruction by building weapons and encouraging wars in order to follow their work ethic or "gospel of success." He asks these captains of fortune whether their labor for money at the cost of human life will being peace for their souls. Such men are pampered in luxury and honor while the tools of human slaughter are unleashed upon the world.

In "Subterranean Homesick Blues" the rock poet grasps the mindless trap offered by the work routine to the young people. The average young person who is fortunate enough to get his undergraduate degree is often faced with the impossible situation of being able to do nothing. He may stand in the tradition of the young man recently depicted in Mike Nichols' film production of *The Graduate*. He has passed the hurdles of education to find himself neither desiring work nor being prepared to do it. His future is a series of options which seem to end in being "plastics."

The plight of the helpless worker is depicted often in this literature. The worker endures the burden of labor in order that he might be real man in his leisure time. John Lennon in "A Hard Day's Night" writes of such a worker:

> It's been a Hard Day's Night
> And I've been working like a dog
> It's been a Hard Day's Night
> I should be sleeping like a log
> But when I get home to you

I find the thing that you do
Will make me feel alright
You know I work all day
To get you money to buy you things[9]

His meaningful life is outside of the job. The labor of his days is just a means for the happiness of the evenings. There is humor and a bit of bite in "Lovely Rita." In this song Lennon comments on the strange nature of today's jobs and the love of a meter maid:

Standing by a parking meter,
When I caught a glimpse of Rita,
Filling in a ticket in her little white book.
In a cap she looked much older,
And the bag across her shoulder
Made her look a little like a military man.[10]

The rock writer conveys an opinion that there is a quality of depersonalization and masculinity about this modern occupation for women. Beatle George Harrison, striking at another of the roots of modern man's work problems, despairs in his song about taxes, "Taxman."

Let me tell you how it will be:
There's one for you nineteen for me.
'Cos I'm the taxman, yeh,
I'm the taxman.
If you drive a truck I'll tax the street,
if you try to fix it, I'll tax your seat.
If you get too cold I'll tax the heat,
if you take a walk I'll tax your feet.
Taxman! And you're working
for no one but me.[11]

In "Paperback Writer" John Lennon describes the hack writers of this day who function only according to public supply and needs:

Dear Sir or Madam will you read my book?
It took me years to write, will you take a look?

Based on a novel by a man Lear and I need a job
so I want to be a paperback writer, paperback writer.[12]

It is a heartless job in which no meaning is found. Paul Simon
extends this judgment of such workers to the realm of poetry
and music. In "Homeward Bound" we find the weary performer
far from home and passing his performances off as merely
functional labor. He does another one-night stand. A new audience pays to see him work at making them believe that he
means what he says. He tries to perform. However, the words
and phrases seem to hang without direction or meaning. The
music fits and the music is played correctly, but it is wrong.
The worker's spirit is elsewhere. He wishes to be where his
love waits. The meaning and the direction to his work dwell
in the harmony of his love. He must not labor in such dishonesty. He must go home.

Again in "Kathy's Song" Simon contrasts the meaning of
work, even artistic work, with the meaning given to life by
love. The writer of a song works but cannot accomplish anything. Time is invested and motions are made. The product
of his labor cannot be authentic. With a forced unnatural style he
mechanically makes words and music fit. Without love they do
not become songs or true fruits of honest labor. The love of this
girl is the only source of life's meaning for the poetry of this
song.

Even the clergyman is seen against a background of meaningless work in "Eleanor Rigby":

Father McKenzie writing the words
of a sermon that no one will hear,
no one comes near.
Look at him working,
darning his socks in the night
when there's nobody there . . .
what does he care?[13]

The humanistic zest to live and enjoy life offers the alternative
to meaningless labor. "What does man gain by all the toil at
which he toils under the sun?" (Eccles. 1:3).

6

The Anti-War Generation: "Kill for Peace"

An old movie theater in the Greenwich Village area of New York City was filled to capacity. This crowd had not come to see films. The crowd—mainly young people—waited in anticipation for a rock stage show in the new home of "Fugs." Finally the curtains opened to display a group of hippy types with their standard rock instruments. Ed Saunders carried much of the show as lead singer. The background music to the songs was rock with a nice freedom to seek effects. However, the lyrics were something else. These musician-poets produced literate compositions which assaulted the virgin ears of a public unaccustomed to this language. The songs described what most of the *now* and *other* generations have seen, felt, or experienced but which they rarely mention. Some refer to their music as "crotch rock."

The show was stopped by enthusiastic applause, not for this free speech material, but for a marvelously bitter statement on war entitled "Kill for Peace." One member of the Fugs wore an American helmet, which was brushed off at the end of the number to reveal a Nazi headpiece beneath. It is hard to know the power of this anti-war statement without hearing the driving beat which compels the listener to feel more and more ready to kill. The Fugs set forth youth's problem with a war for peace when the enemies and the reasons for killing are not clear:

Kill, Kill, Kill for peace
Kill, Kill, Kill for peace

If you don't like a people
or the way they talk
If you don't like their manners
or the way they walk,
Kill, Kill, Kill for peace
Kill, Kill, Kill for peace

. . . . . .

If you let them live they may
subvert the Prussians into
If you let them live they might
love the Russians,
Kill, Kill, Kill for peace
Kill 'em, kill 'em, strafe them, goop creeps

. . . . . .

Kill, it will give you the mental ease
Kill, it will give you a big release.[1]

Eric Berne, in his discussion of transactional analysis, depicts the action of interpersonal relationships as serious "games." "A game is an ongoing series of complementary ulterior transactions progressing to a well-defined outcome."[2] He calls war the grimmest of all. The naked reasons and absurdity of war are comprehended by the *now* generation. The pursuit of peace through killing catches man in contradiction to his spiritual being. War to the young is a grim game hidden behind the foliage of dishonesty concerning man's purpose of love and fulfillment.

Many of those comprising the *now* generation are caught in the absurdity of this. In a time when living could be so wonderful, men seek death. An African student attending school in this country expresses the burden on the minds of the young facing war as he writes from his wonder of the beauty of America: "Sir, one thing bothers me—how many of us are going to survive this World War III? I have a zest to live and I hope the giant governments realize that." It has been most unfortunate that some of the *other* generation have equated such sensitivity and questioning about our war policy with the killing of the troops in Vietnam. The wellspring of the longing for peace in the face of so much killing is the same from which the strongest hawk also is nurtured.

The Christian tradition is inseparable from a search to make peace rather than war. It is useless to produce biblical texts to prove such an assumption. The game can be played on both sides. However, the impact of Christ upon men is one which makes each person seriously face the question of non-violence. With Peter, man is tempted to beat off the "bad guys" with a sword, but Christ seemed to accept the means of his capture, torture, and destruction at the hands of evil men as justified by the end: the resurrection (John 18:10-11). It is so difficult to establish an ethical position in relation to killing. There seem to be so many personal examples of situations which would seem to justify killing for protection against aggression.

This is the point of confusion for the generation faced with the actual fighting. They can understand how Dietrich Bonhoeffer, the martyred German pastor and theologian, could find himself making the decision to participate in a plot on the life of Hitler and thereby advocating assassination. However, many young people have difficulty when it comes to rationalizing our action in Vietnam. The young of today cannot accept the thoughtless nationalism of the past: "I am with my country, right or wrong." As Christians and as Americans, they must understand and make a commitment only to those positions which are right and consistent with the Christian conscience.

It is a bit embarrassing to discuss war with those deeply opposed to the Asian involvement of the United States and have them continually come back to theological reasons for their anti-war position. It is distressing because such thinking comes from those *outside* the organized church! On the other hand, one often finds those within the church supporting the government's actions without any theological questioning at all.

The Second City Players express what is uncomfortably close to youth's impression of the strange position of the church in the matter of war. In the skit, a newsman is interviewing an officer who has been sent to Vietnam as an adviser to train

South Vietnamese troops. He explains that his biggest problem is the fact that the people are Buddhist and don't believe in killing. He feels that there is one ray of hope to change this: Christianity is catching on! Our young people will continue to go to war. A few, a very few will catch the attention of the news media as they articulate the undercurrent of questioning about the morality of this war and war in general. Rock music at a number of points reflects this theological concern of the age.

Arlo Guthrie's monologue on ethics and war, "Alice's Restaurant Massacree," is a caricature of the conflict between the immorality of war and the morals of society. He tells the meandering story of a young man who gets fined for littering. This act of misdirected zeal to clean a friend's house is treated with great seriousness by the police. He later visits the induction center to get his physical with great enthusiasm. He tells the psychologist that he wants to shoot down and destroy the enemy with his bare hands. His patriotic rage forces him to jump up and down with bloody fury. He is a ready-made killing machine. The army is pleased with this potential soldier until they find that he has been charged with a crime: littering. At this point Arlo underscores the inconsistencies created by war as he confronts the induction officer with the ironic fact that he is being judged too immoral to kill. His criminal activity as a litterbug makes him unfit for the service. The army will not allow one who throws paper on the ground to be part of a force which lays down destruction upon innocent women and children, farms and towns, friend and enemy. He is finally rejected by the army because of his immorality.

War infects every nation, every religion, and every age. The wars of the past have not excluded the possibility of war in the future. In fact, war never seems to end war. The victory of one conflict is the seed of tomorrow's battle. It is the universal soldier in each tradition, in each human body, which must be put to rest.

The impracticability and idealism of the Christian tradition as preserved in the teaching material of Matthew 5-7 is consistent with youth's thrust for truth without the price of a lie:

You have heard that it was said, "An eye for an eye and a tooth for a tooth." But I say to you, Do not resist one who is evil. But if any one strikes you on the right cheek, turn to him the other also . . . (Matt. 5:38-40).

Whether this idealistic segment of the culture is realistic in its search for such peace without death is for every man to decide. It is clear that many have been led by insights drawn from the theological tradition which has opposed war and killing.

A statement of the uneasiness that exists between a commitment to the Prince of Peace or to the war is seen in Paul Simon's arrangement of "Silent Night." Simon and Garfunkel sing this Christmas carol against the background of the 7 o'clock news. A report of Richard Nixon's plea for more troops in the Asian conflict jars the serenity of that quiet night of hope. Can these two activities of the mind, spirit, and flesh be compatible: the Christian life and war? Perhaps this tension is our last hope, and we should be thankful for it. To the rock generation, the nature of the confrontation between faith and dishonest living is acute. Every age has had this realization that things are taught one way and done another. However, the *now* generation wants theory and method to be consistent. It may choose to fight, but it also may choose to oppose war and still love country, faith, and truth.

The early Dylan material is particularly sensitive to the uneasy balance between war and peace. In "Masters of War" he strikes out in the direction of the "they" who have made this mess. It is not the blind indictment against a generation in power which gives the song such bite. Bob Dylan attacks the reasons or philosophy behind their actions. He writes of the American's obsession with the molding of the young's opinion of our "enemies." It is hatred of people unknown and unseen which fans the flames of future wars. The Russians are often depicted by radical patriots as being guilty of every crime. They surely must eat babies. These masters of war are seen as teaching the youth that war can be won, and then they flee to let young blood flow. The cost of such training in hatred and fear is staggering. In one of his album cover poems Dylan writes of this.

The hatred of enemies is one of man's noblest rationalizations for fighting and killing. The simple Bible verse from Sunday school days is mashed by the cold world machinery to read: "Love *some* of your enemies" (Matt. 5:44). The lines of this Dylan poem underscore the young generation's awareness that the hatred developed for the purpose of war leads to self-destruction.

How can man, being honest, devote himself to hating a people beyond his personal relationship when the real teeth of rats bite the legs and arms of sleeping babies here and now? The fruits of such misdirected hate toward distant enemies at the expense of the local rat-control ripened in the eyes of the young generation during the summers of 1967 and 1968. With the Asian war costs escalating in terms of human life and money, Congress in early 1967 refused to launch a local war against the millions of rats inhabiting the major cities of America. In the summers of rioting which followed, military troops had to be used against our own rat-infested people. The lack of understanding toward these problems by our political leadership is ably matched by the church's embarrassing failure to understand the younger generation. Government leaders from both parties demonstrated to the youth of America their misreading of war and peace, home and abroad, when they used the riots as an excuse to attack the other party.

Yet, youth bears the undeniable stamp of the *other* generation's teaching. The burden of prejudice and malice scars the young and makes the process of love and understanding for others outside youth's experience so much harder. For such a destructive distortion of human nature the rock poet can see no forgiveness, as in his song "Masters of War." It is the judgment of the young outside the establishment church that the men behind war could never be forgiven. Dylan further comments on the *other* generation's support of this "game" of destruction in "With God on Our Side." Each verse presents another example of our nation's long history of bloody wars with its intense development of new hatreds for enemies real and imagined. We justify such activity by thinking that this nation is godly and the enemy is wicked.

H. Rap Brown, former chairman of the Student Non-Violent

Co-ordinating Committee, shocked America when he reportedly said, "Violence is necessary. It is as American as cherry pie." The purpose and principles of our country have not advocated violence, but history and national policy testify to its consistent use. The assassinations of John F. Kennedy, Malcolm X, Dr. Martin Luther King, Jr., and Senator Robert F. Kennedy have vividly occurred within the short life span of the *now* generation. Bloody wars have been waged among our own people and with others. How does one teach the poor or the young that everything can happen through due process of law and order when the history of our nation reveals that violence is the means by which things are really accomplished in the American tradition? How do we proclaim love and peace to the poor and the young when we are doing all in our power to have Americans hate the Russians and Chinese? Are the poor to be told to be patient and law-abiding while those who are affluent offer their unquestioning support to the military task of village-by-village destruction of people in another land? The young know that something is wrong with this call for both the blood of our enemies and the submission, in meekness, of the rat-bitten and mistreated poor.[3] The lingering questions remain for the *other* generation and particularly for the church to hear and respond to.

The confusion is heightened when the young observe a shift in the society's objects of hatred. Perhaps some of them have seen world war. Who are the bad guys? Some of the younger generation still remember the government film which was produced during a time when the Russians were considered our friends. Friendly and industrious people, the Russians looked much like Americans in that film. But times change and they are now enemies. Perhaps the government will soon make another policy change and have them depicted as friends again, with a new enemy replacing them as an object of hatred. Have these peoples changed or has our self-interest dictated whether they will be loved or destroyed? These are the kinds of questions which seem so puzzling to those who want to live with zest and love without war.

In "Let Me Die in My Footsteps" Dylan again captures the

desire of man to die naturally rather than while living in a shelter underground.

The acceptance by small children that the world stands on the brink of nuclear destruction and that bomb shelters are needed seems wrong. People should be seeking new dimensions of living, instead of thinking about ways of death. The ground is a place for footsteps. It should not be a blanket for premature death through war.

Janis Ian experiences this same tainting of nature by the cold war gift of imminent destruction. In "Bahimsa" she sings of the earth prone in death by war:

> And when a wind from Hiroshima
> blows ashes
> into the town
> When they slowly sift and form
> a blanket
> upon the ground
> When the earth turns to a tomb
> no flowers
> can be found . . .[4]

The flowers of life have become the flowers for graves. War and life cannot co-exist. The love of life is being covered by the popularity of war's death. Man surrenders his humanity for inhumanity. The witness of these statements on war and its dehumanizing qualities is represented well in the Simon-Garfunkel composition "Scarborough Fair/Canticle," where the writers give us the context in which the young look at war and killing. The simple and joyous quality of a lovely young girl and the sensual awareness of the spices clash with the soldier's summons to leave this love, prepare his weapon of destruction, and follow an older person's order to be a killer. The cause and the reasoning behind this journey of death have been distorted or lost for a long time. The haunting hymnlike quality of this song provides a striking contrast to the madness of war for a person who would rather live and love.

The Beatles and most of the other groups comprising the

representatives of the rock scene have an interest in an anti-war commitment. Within the past few years the Beatles and others have gone elsewhere as the *now* generation's poets have taken the subterranean route and tried to explore man's internal needs and strengths. There is a sense of reality about life, love, and war in the writings of these composers. They do not accept the unalterability of war as being right or good. In fact, John Lennon expressed his despair with man's glorification of war by starring in Richard Lester's controversial anti-war film, *How I Won the War*. The absurd is used to prick man's heroic rationalization of human destruction.

The rock writers experientially grasp a doctrine of sinful man in a sinful society. Yet, they know the possibility and reality of love among persons as persons. The humanistic affirmation of this generation is clearly the positive source of opposition to war.

The rock poets reflect the theological concerns of the youth of our times. The quest they are undertaking is both an acceptance and a rejection of the world. This means that there are not many anti-war songs as such among the current materials. However, the attempts to rebuild life in the midst of loneliness and alienation from others with the tools of love is perhaps the strongest action against war.

The biblical material often referred to as the Sermon on the Mount (Matthew 5-7) has a strange and fascinating appeal to the *now* generation. The person who drops out of society by trying to turn the other cheek or to go the second mile is spiritually close to one aspect of the early church. The hippies are a portion of an anti-war generation who are simply enacting that which has roots deep within the *other* generation and within the Christian faith itself.

It is hard for the *other* generation to encounter the many faces of youth's anti-war concern. One means of expressing this sentiment is provided by the anti-war pickets who, with their alien flags or quiet resignation, aggressively startle the senses to an awareness of what's happening. There is danger in such overt expressions of protest. Janis Ian warns many about the real motives behind such a challenge of society in her song "Honey D'Ya Think":

> your all against the Vietnam war
> you make it plain
> you would go to all the marches
> in an ecstasy of faith
> but you couldn't spare a quarter
> for a blind man on a corner[5]

The young demand protest stemming from love for humanity. The phony element is among the marchers. However, it does not represent the deep affirmation for life which is behind the strong anti-war concerns of youth.

By dropping out, the hippies shockingly state another reaction to the evil of war. With love of persons and cool rejection of society's senseless habit of destruction, they unnerve older people who are not accustomed to seeing convictions leading behavior.

The third, and most accepted, avenue of anti-war expression is reflected in the countless faces of the young in the newsreels as they fight in a distant land and have their bodies returned to cemeteries in every small town in America. They went and died without voicing a complaint, but why did they give their lives for killing when they could have loved and lived with and for others?

The forms of media used by the young who question war are often jarring to a generation used to its morality in print and on pages. The generation of the rock writers may speak through song, picket signs, or even buttons ("Make love, not war." "War is good business, invest your son").

However, the *now* generation is serving a prophetic ministry to our age with its questioning about war and life. The rock poets are expressive voices crying for others to hear.

Youth's Rebellion Against Society: "These Men Who Have Turned the World Upside Down . . ." (Acts 17:6)

A few days after the annual exodus of students from the university, several campus ministers were enjoying an evening of good conversation about the past year's experience. One pastor, who had captured the imagination and hearts of the whole campus community in his work, was sharing the changes that had taken place in his view of the immediate generation and in his relationship to it.

> When I first started preparing myself for this work, I pictured myself either a Dostoyevsky character such as Prince Myshkin in *The Idiot* or a Mary Poppins. I would go to the young people of today and help this band of misdirected innocents become sensitive to the outcasts of society with the goal of having them do good works.

He stopped to draw certain conclusions in his mind and continued,

> After the past few years of experience I feel more like a Saul Alinsky, a catalyst in enabling the students to become effectively organized to rebel against the whole direction of higher education and society. Perhaps my task is both.

The process of rebellion against the past is the very continuity which is the history of the human experience. Youth's internalization of the past in order to make it its own involves a certain destruction of form and, sometimes, of content. The process of desecularizing that which was holy in the past would have been called by the Greeks the "forward thrust" which insures the continuation of the race. Rebellion, when viewed from the perspective of history, must be acknowledged as being important and valid. A historical perspective of America reveals a great debt to the manifestation of rebellion. In the areas of politics (formation of our nation), economics (a living wage for workers), and social relationships (women's rights and the beginning of Black rights), it might be observed that progressive developments come only with the aid of open rebellion.

It is quite another thing to be personally at the cutting edge of this drama of change. There is a telling scene in the film *Viva Zapata!* in which the rebel leader, played by Marlon Brando, subjects a peasant to the same kind of harassment he once received from former leaders for raising the same questions. He suddenly sees what has happened: the revolution is now the status quo with the same attitudes as the former administration! This shock of recognition is often shielded from those participating in the drama of life. The noble liberal white seems to be quite at home in the civil rights picture until he finds that he cannot comfortably talk with the emerging militant Black leaders who call for new directions. At that moment, the pinch of rebellion falls upon those who once rebelled. To take liberties with a handy axiom, it could be observed, "Scratch a liberal and you will find an enemy."[1] Parents often participate in the process of rebellion on the side which receives the emotional blows inflicted by the rebels. It hurts the *other* generation to be confronted by the signs which reveal discontent with its values and accomplishments.

The Christian faith has a long history of facing theological rebellion from within and from without. Jesus troubled the religious people of his day. The accounts of his words and mission are preserved as a continuity with the past, yet the established generation of the day could see the seeds of rebellion being sown. The generation called forth by Christ to take the gospel to the world became people who "turned the world upside down" (Acts 17:6).

The second-century Gnostic fathers called for a new orientation concerning Christ, the Scriptures, life, and death. The church battled for its life against the mystical speculation of these heretical sects. The theological establishment which won the battle was changed by the intellectual encounter with the Gnostic challenge. The Roman Empire could resist the rebellion of Christianity until it incorporated the movement within its official body. The church then had to rebel anew against the restrictions which came with this manifestation of the faith.

The age of the Reformation is an example of a dramatic manifestation of God's people facing rebellion. The splits within the body left both sides changed by the encounters and struggle. The elements which developed out of the rebellion against Rome soon hardened to a new orthodoxy which opened it to many of the criticisms originally aimed at the Church of Rome.

The modern Christian must try to understand this process of change as being normative for the Christian faith and society. Man must accept for himself, sometimes in very different ways, the commitment which is faith and life. Society in continuity is actually reconstituted more rapidly than each biological generation. It is clear that the generations in the age of mass media will become even more rapidly isolated. More subcultures will be recognized within each age span. This isolation and demarcation of subgenerations will be heightened by market research in advertising and mass media programming attempts to find special markets and audiences. Products will be developed to mark a subculture and create its needs. This suggests even more rebellion from each subculture against demands made upon them from other subcultures.

The most revealing comment a person can make in his evaluation of the standards of another subculture is to say, "That is too far out." Such an admission glaringly admits the burning pain of change and rebellion. This age, as it rebels, is kicking over the values and thought patterns of the past as it rebels. The rock music of this generation manifests this reaction against society.

The younger generation can feel the cost of its rebellion.

Tension, rejection, and the open retaliation by society against rebellion are all familiar to the rock generation. In some cases, young people reveal the belief that this hostility is similar to that experienced by the early Christians. There is something promising in conflict over values, ideals, and change. Both sides gain if they allow honest dialogue to simply unfold. Bob Dylan speaks for many when he reports some of the older generation's impossible groping for the mystery of change in "The Ballad of a Thin Man." Something is happening in the young's dissatisfaction with the injustice and destruction in life. The adults can feel something moving in the world of the *now* generation. They don't, however, understand what is going on. The man who does not know what is happening in rebellion cannot communicate or understand what is sought. To so many adults, the restlessness and rebellion of the young is beyond understanding. "Don't they have everything they need?" The times are changing and the static norms for judging moving ideas are wrong.

Youth can understand the hostile reactions to their quest to overcome the structured order. Many of those who now hold power were once the rebels against another order in another time. Some of the older generation resent their own loss of freedom, or inclination to rebel, in exchange for security and acceptance. Dylan expresses this plight in "It's Alright, Ma."

John Lennon writes in "Nowhere Man" of a person caught in the structure of society, who has released his mind, heart, and emotions to the whims of daily pressure. The nowhere everyman is "a bit like you and me." This is the prototype person who must face the decision of being for or against the organization of the world. There is here the sad realization that maturation brings acceptance and a surrender of rebellion in most people.

There are those also who have quietly forsaken the rebellion of the past and do not realize it. John Lennon comically characterizes such a person of either generation in "Getting Better":

> It's getting better all the time
> I used to get mad at my school

The teachers that taught me weren't cool
You're holding me down, turning me round
Filling me up with your rules.
I've got to admit it's getting better.
A little better all the time[2]

This state of rebellion does change and will come again with
the next *now* generations. Lennon slyly notes that the rebellious
spirit of one time becomes the status quo in another when he
writes in "When I'm Sixty-Four":

We shall scrimp and save
Grandchildren on your knee
Vera, Chuck & Dave
Send me a postcard, drop me a line,
Stating point of view
Indicate precisely what you mean to say
Yours sincerely, wasting away
Give me your answer, fill in a form
Mine for evermore
Will you still need me, will you still feed me.
When I'm sixty-four.[3]

Such delusion sends chills into the marrow of most young people.
Will they also be bought and delivered as they become the
other generation and no longer know the growing edge of
change?

One image is used by a number of our rock writers to sym-
bolize the *now* generation's means of rebelling. Dylan, Ian, and
Simon allude to "writings" on unexpected places. This means of
rebellion is found in the biblical tradition. Belshazzar, the Bab-
ylonian king, flouted the God of Israel only to be confronted
by a mysterious inscription which appeared on the wall to judge
his scandalous behavior (Dan. 5:1-31). Jesus writes in the sand
as a response to those who self-righteously would execute a girl
caught in sin (John 8:2-11). His rebellious writing in the dust
turns the crowd's lust for blood to an admission of their own
sins. The combination of the reverent and irreverent on walls is

rebelliously reflected in the decorations of ancient Jewish worship buildings excavated in Dura which have pagan pictures representing religious stories!

The rock poets provide continuity with these past examples of profane rebellion. Dylan can see such creative rebellion on the walls of unlikely places as the real sites for art:

> Art, if there is such a thing, is in the bathrooms; everybody knows that. To go to an art-gallery thing . . . That's just a status affair. I'm not putting it down, mind you; but I spend a lot of time in the bathroom. I think museums are vulgar.[4]

Paul Simon writes of a man who must enact his rebellion against society in a deserted subway tunnel with "A Poem on the Underground Wall." The underground rebel against society's structure quickly draws a crayon from his coat. He chooses a billboard and boldly prints a four-letter word. It is "love" or something more startling. Why does he rebel in this hidden way? Such a frustrated attempt to make a rebellious statement concerning society is quite widespread and perhaps creative. A recent study of graffiti, or writing on walls, shows the striking range of rebellion expressed in this secret form of overturning the accepted.[5] Paul Simon in "The Sound of Silence,"* captures the danger of such a silent rebellion by predicting a world which confines self-expression to random walls:

> And the sign flashed out its warning.
> In the words that it was forming,
> And the signs said "The words of the prophets
> are written on the subway walls
> and tenement halls"[6]

Janis Ian also speaks of the danger in such use of the rebellious means of communication in "New Christ Cardiac Hero":

> Your lectures of ways are only today's poolroom jokes
> Scrawled on the walls of tenement halls and bathroom
>   bowls.[7]

---

* "The Sound of Silence" by Paul Simon. © 1964 & 1965 by Charing Cross Music. Used with permission of the publisher.

Youth raises the important question of the nature of rebellion. When does it come as a constructive means of changing society and when does it remain simpleminded whining? They also raise the question of man's nature as a rebelling person when he must resort to hidden forms of putting the cry for change on the wall. How does one discern valid rebellion and that which will last beyond the initial indignation? Do not the walled words of rebellion insult some in every age? Must not the young and old realize that to some a four-letter word on a wall will be obscene while to others it may be a commentary of life as seen by the rebel?

The idealism natural to youth often views the act or thought of rebellion as quite noble. In "The Chimes of Freedom" Dylan speaks of the bells ringing for those who have rebelled, challenged society, failed, and been punished. It is right and proper that one should challenge society. The cost may be steep, but for some this is the price of human dignity.

There is, however, a clear enough picture of reality in the rock literature to see that being a rebel against society is going to cost. In "Rainy Day Women #12 and #35" Bob Dylan reflects the inner peace and sense of humor the rebel must have when facing society. If he does what he must do in the name of truth, he will have the scorn of society cast upon him. In fact, Dylan claims that one will be punished by stoning no matter what he attempts to do. It must be accepted in good spirit. No matter what a person does society will stone him. This is also good biblical tradition (i.e., Jesus, Stephen, and Paul). Rebellion in life is the joyous struggle of continually becoming a new person in a world which punishes changes.

The *now* generation sees society as composed of people who are struggling to become persons. It is also a subculture which realizes that injustice and evil reside in the structure and organization of society. The investment of tradition in the body of social institutions and structures results in forces being created to resist rebellion and change. The young harbor a deep animosity toward such structures which often seem to exist just to resist change.

Paul Simon uses the image of the zoo as being expressive of the rigid structures surrounding social convention. In "At the Zoo"* we find a microcosm of society:

> Something tells me,
> it's all happening At The Zoo.
> I do believe it.
> I do believe it's true.
> The monkeys stand for honesty,
> Giraffes are insincere,
> And the elephants are kindly,
> but they're dumb.
> Orangutans are skeptical
> of changes in their cages,
> And the zookeeper is very fond of rum.[8]

The stratification of society is captured at the zoo. How does one successfully rebel against the neat value structures given by the family and the other social institutions? How does the young person really make a decision about that which is different when he has been told the experience or person is bad? How can a college student answer a question about the possibility of having a roommate of another race when he has no personal experience, but only the opinions of the *other* generation upon which to base his decision?

"Society's Child" is the form through which Janis Ian is able to express youth's frustration in the face of having to choose between an interracial dating situation and what the structure says. The mother in the song tells the daughter, "But, honey, he's not our kind." The peer group, the teachers, and the proclaimers of equality will not let the two young people continue their relationship. In the closing lines of this statement on youth's defeated rebellion, she writes:

> When we're older things may change.
> But for now this is the way they must remain.
> I say I can't see you anymore, baby,

---

* "At the Zoo" by Paul Simon. © 1967 by Paul Simon. Used with permission of the publisher.

Can't see you anymore.
No, I don't want to see you anymore, baby.[9]

Can such patterns of structure and mind-set really be resisted
by the rebels of this age? Will she ever rebel? It is not just the
structures which are forbidding and destructive. How sad it is to
recognize those who can mouth the words and feel the emotions,
but lack the courage to be the rebel they are called to be. This
generation of rebellion acutely faces a point of decision. Young
people are being challenged by the times to assert their personhood to and with others by bravely facing the battle of rebellion presented by society. Many are choosing to rebel.

In the song "Patterns," Paul Simon raises the question of
youth being caught in a structure of life which is overwhelming.
The *now* generation often feels that it is a laboratory experimental rat. A patterned path has been set before each person.
It must be followed. The options are few and the course cannot
be changed. Even death is mapped out in advance. Arlo Guthrie
well reflects the rebel in a more philosophical moment in his
song "I'm Going Home." Man is caught in a cycle which traps
all living things. He rebels and then accepts that which he must:

> Once a man he lived and died
> what he said death could not hide
> even tho' it is often tried
> but he was going home
> Now my friends, it's time to go
> and this love will live to grow
> and I want you ought to know
> I am going home[10]

It isn't blind fate which encompasses the youth in these songs.
It is society's control of the changeable factors of life which
keeps men in their separate boxes. Even within the structures of
life the rebel has a chance to be himself. A true man lives for
others. When his rest comes, it will be peace.

Fired on by a deep sense of man finding his humanity, the
now generation has been captivated by the crude injustice of

the racial situation in this country. It has been the youth of America who have at least been responsible for breaking up the logjam in the flood of racial justice which has been damming up the stream of American life for 300 years. The kids who have been rebelling on the pavement with their marches, at lunch counters with their bodies, and through tutoring programs with their personal concern have changed the course of American history. This has *not* been done just to raise hell. The youth's commitment of self for others has been undertaken as rebellion against the inhumanity of this society. The kids on the front lines of struggle for the restoration of dignity are there as rebels in search of themselves and are supporting the other person's quest for his dignity.

Dylan's words have expressed much about the reasons for the early student work in the rebellion against discrimination. In "Only a Pawn in Their Game" he pinpoints the blame for the Southern death struggle in the direction of those in authority. The politician has traditionally found it useful to keep the poor whites in fear of the poor blacks. They feed the areas of ignorance and pride to make the shanty whites feel superior to someone. They are being used like pawns in some horrible game of death. The forces of hatred and injustice must be overthrown. The work against racial injustice is not a movement or organization as such. It's the spirit of freedom—an ideal, whose time is at hand. Bob Dylan rightly discerns the rebellion of the spirit which is upon us. A wind is blowing across the land which cannot be turned back. It is a breeze which restores human dignity. Whatever the cost of this new realization of man's right to be free, it will be paid. This wind or spirit is the theological breeze catching the imagination and hearts of this rebellious time. It is not the property of the church or even organized religion. For some, this spirit of rebelling for the sake of another's humanity is Christ become flesh. In the words of those who feared at another time when the Spirit of God seemed to be moving among people where they were and not where it was expected: "You see that you can do nothing; look, the world has gone after him" (John 12:19).

The rebellion of the current age is directly related to this time and this people. How well will the *now* generation fare when it has become entrenched with its successful rebellion and is being besieged by the new troops? The rock music of today will also be challenged when times change. The past will then seem to some to be pushing at the rebellious perimeter of the structures which must pass.

Artist Sister Mary Corita, who combines the pop art scene with the theological quest, often creates in her silk-screen prints the moment of encounter where life and gospel meet. In one of them she ably combines the terror of the Watts riot, as reported on the front page of the *Los Angeles Times*, with the words of Maurice Oulett concerning change and rebellion:

> Youth is a time of rebellion. Rather than squelch the rebellion, we might better enlist the rebels to join that greatest rebel of his time—Christ Himself.

Some Personal Afterthoughts:
"Surely This Is Not Without Meaning . . ."

Jim was one of the last high school students to leave the Sunday school class. He put his arm around the college sophomore who taught the twenty-five young people and said, "Benson, baby, you make it painless Christianity." The teacher was a bit concerned by this remark. Did this mean that by being colorful and informal he had failed in getting the religious material across? The church had conditioned this inexperienced teacher with an unspoken sense that religious teaching should not be described as being interesting and enjoyable.

The implications gained from a serious dialogue with the youth subculture are personally disturbing to one who is both a son of the church and a fan of youth culture. In general, the church and today's youth seem to have retreated from one another. Each demands allegiance to his thought patterns alone. When there is a hopeful sign of someone "being where the kids are," his peer group is suspicious of his methods. Sometimes he is even prevented from continuing his work with youth when such leadership breaks with the *other* generation's restricted orientation. Creative work with youth or adults is simply not nurtured by the church in most places.

There are four aspects of youth culture which particularly speak to the modern church: (1) consistency between media and content; (2) rebellion and irreverence; (3) humanistic concerns; and (4) experiential zest.

1. Consistency Between Media and Content: "Tell It the Way It Is, Baby"

It is a bit frightening to think about what is happening to those young people who are learning about the person and mission of Christ while being captive audiences in church basements on Sunday mornings. They know that it is not "painless Christianity." George Orwell commented on the future of colonial Africa in 1939 as he caught a disturbing restlessness in the eyes of the native porters who learned the merits of Western civilization by bearing European rifles to kill other Africans for Europeans. The writer and essayist speculated about the children raised on inconsistencies in every age, when he wrote:

> How much longer can we go on kidding these people?
> How long before they turn their guns in the other direction?[1]

How long will it be before the silent Sunday morning army of youth realize what poor fare it has been fed and will turn from the church?

The implications of the rock generation's concern for the relationship between form and substance, persons and teachings, often put the large church in a bad light. Tradition and analogy to business often tempt the big religious institution to become an inflexible organization. There is often the "great" preacher and then there are minor staff members, who do the "other" ministries. If such a church took seriously the continuity or inseparability of form and content, it would be faced with a very different structural nature in the staff ministries. The fragmentation and resulting value judgments placed on the different staff ministries of the large church need to be overcome in order to convey the unity of Christ's body to the people.

The structure of the church, influenced by this aspect of youth culture, should be flexible to reflect the church's content: God's people at worship, study, fellowship, and service. The results awakened by a new sensitivity to people would then be colorful, striking, and capable of pulling people out of themselves with odors, sights, touch, and sound. The process would begin with the rediscovery of the Word of God at the point where the people were.

The worship act in a *now* generation church would be the enactment of the drama of salvation with the whole staff participating. It would be a service in which there would not be *a* leader.

An example of this kind of team leadership of worship was enacted when two pastors returned from participating in a public demonstration for an open occupancy law in Milwaukee.[2] One pastor agreed to share in the other's worship service. They wanted to convey the spirit of their witness for justice with others through the act of corporate worship. The next day happened to be Worldwide Communion Sunday, a day celebrated by Protestants throughout the world.

On the following day, the two pastors led the service together. When they reached the portion of the service for the administration of the Sacrament, the host pastor talked about the unity which brought all Christians to the Lord's Table on that particular Sunday. He paused to wonder aloud if it were really unity of opinion which invited them all to this Sacrament. At that point the other pastor stood beside the host minister and they both removed their robes. Beneath the pastoral garments one minister wore a sweatshirt which read "NAACP Youth Council. We love Father Groppi." The other pastor revealed a shirt which read "KKK. We hate Father Groppi."

They then marched around the communion table shouting at each other. One yelled bitter comments about bigots and the other about those who marched in the streets. They stopped at each end of the table. The anti-civil rights character poured out a string of bitter comments about the kind of people represented by the person at the other end of the table. When he had finished, the other participant bitterly attacked the first speaker with harsh words.

The two men paused in their heated exchange. The man identified as the bigot confessed that he was not filled only with hate. He asserted that he would never change his mind about civil rights, but he did wish that he could understand the man at the other end of the table. The activist in turn confessed that his indignation often blinded him from knowing the persons he opposed. While he would not change his view on civil rights, he, too, wished that he could relate to the other.

They then both stepped behind the Table. One pastor assured the congregation that the band of men which Christ gathered around the Table disagreed over who should have honor and even what loyalty to Christ meant. Yet, Christ fed them in order that they might have the assurance that in him they would always be one. After the pastors had shared in the words of Institution and the people had communed, they passed the peace to each other and to the people.

A man stopped to speak with the host pastor at the door. He had been a vocal critic of the church's involvement in social issues. He thanked the pastor for sharing with him another way to look at the whole matter.

Who led the service? Who was the preacher? Two men were able to be vessels by which the people could experience a reality often absent in the usual personality-centered worship experience.

The fluidity and freshness of the worship act could be so constructed that the people would see continuity between form and content. The people would see by the interrelationships of the staff in the worship experience a symbol of the unity in Christ's body. This would be an experience. The senses would be assaulted with the "good news" of Christ. With the unexpected and fresh would be the familiar from the past. The Word would be spoken and enacted with new music, art, drama, and participation.

For example, even the implements used in worship should relate the content to the people.[3] The usual Sunday bulletin with its cover picture of the church building would seem out of place. The inexpensive process of making mimeograph stencils electronically could be utilized to reproduce newspaper photographs. The worshiper would experience a visual relationship between human need and God's love. Even further exploration of relating form and content could lead to this graphic dimension of worship being moved from the cover of the bulletin to the inside. The liturgy could be printed around or over a striking photograph.

Even a congregation's desire to use hymns of questionable theology or relevance would now be seen in a new perspective. A series of striking slides could be projected on the wall during the singing of these familiar hymns. The implicit meanings of the lyrics could be underscored or questioned through impressive visuals.

A church listening to the lessons of youth culture would be strongly sacramental. The symbols of salvation would be a regular part of the worship service at every occasion. Christ taught his disciples at the Last Supper by giving new meaning to that which was common. In the same act he also gave himself to others. Christ would not be denied the people as is generally done now. The comment that regular participation in the Lord's Supper would make it lose its meaning reveals the inadequate worship experience the people are accustomed to receiving.

With staff members and laymen mutually participating in the leadership of worship (not just a prayer for you and a Scripture lesson for her), the people of God would grasp through compatible media and content the mutuality of the Christian life. The whole congregation also would become part of the process of enabling the worship experience to be significant each time people gather.

2. Rebellion and Irreverence: "Yes, But . . ."

A wave of irreverent rebellion faces the world and particularly the church. The young leaders within the church are often discouraged and go elsewhere because the forces of tradition beat them. With the departure of such leadership goes also the last hope of having a meaningful church for this day. Rebellion and disagreement must again be recognized as being healthy for growth. The people of God must learn its oneness and unity through the freedom to rebel and disagree without weakening the basic allegiance to Christ which holds the body together. In *Cry, the Beloved Country*, Alan Paton has expressed man's need for the experience of irreverent rebellion in the church and his disappointment with the inability of the church to allow it. John Kumalo is a political figure who wants a change in the life of his beloved country. The emerging native leadership demands the passing of the outdated tribal structure. The chief, who is the tool of the white man, must be replaced. The new breed of political activist casts a disturbing judgment on the structures which must go:

> It is breaking apart, your tribal society. It is here in Johannesburg that the new society is being built. Something is happening here, my brother.
> He paused for a moment, then he said, I do not wish to offend you gentlemen, but the Church too is like the chief. You must do so and so and so. You are not free to have an experience. A man must be faithful and meek and obedient, and he must obey the laws, whatever the laws may be.[4]

From the mouth of this revolutionary character comes the modern man's indictment of the church in our time. The church allows structures and their preservation to hinder the working of the Holy Spirit. The church has not provided the world with meaningful encounter with God. This is not a plea for emotionalism. The church is simply in an age of fluidity and yet the church remains structurally rigid. The manifestation of a new holiness or reverence out in the world suggests that the church may not be the place for the *now* generation's new faith.

Rock theology summons the church to link the person and mission of Christ directly to the means by which we teach, worship, and live this faith. Content and form must be related. The communicational gap between the generations seems also to be applicable to those within as well as without the church. Such an awareness of the times and its exciting sensuality means that a process of irreverence will have to be accepted by the church. We are justified in challenging everything about the church's past. We must be prepared to strike out irreverently for the new in order to have a holiness which has meaning in our time.

Rebellion in study and worship would undercut and destroy the many vestigial activities which the church carries on its back out of reverence for the past. A church is alive in its quest to overthrow the past. For instance, there would be no need for a conscious social calendar or the women's circle if it did not have a real purpose consistent with the Christian church in our age. The committee meetings with the pastor's canned opening prayer would be replaced with a meaningful expression of worship. The people would discover new meaning in their home worship and carry this back into the church.

Groups within the church's life would be gathered according to interest and not just according to the age clustering of the past. Some high school young people might very well find an interesting study area which also attracts older people. The generational gap would not be widened as the current church programming tends to do.

In such a church large or small, there would be a great respect given to the whole teaching task. It would be the highest honor to be a teacher. Greatest support would be given to the teaching task. Perhaps such an idea as forwarded by Locke Bowman, who proposes a teaching center with modern teaching equipment in place of the kitchen, might be followed.[5]

The rock generation does not speak directly about the mechanics of the church as we know it. However, the youth's concern for building a bridge between what one believes and how he lives is one of the rock generation's gifts to the church. The church under such influence would feel called to be radically obedient and ready to die as a structure in order that Christ might be known.

The organizational church as we know it may well face death and truly become what one churchman has called the "grave of God." The Holy Spirit will continue to manifest itself among these people at the crossroads of suffering, crisis, pain, and love. In some churches, such an attempt to discover themselves has begun. The remnant people who read, study, worship, and serve are drawn to others for such a common life. This house-church or small group movement is sometimes authentic and is the church. People are supported in their rebellion against the meaninglessness by the encounter with others in the task of being the church. There is also great danger in such offshoots of the

church. They can become isolated cells which fall to the same
parochial distortion of the faith as the larger unit. At their best,
these manifestations of the body of Christ reach out and touch
others. They have a life together in common with the response
recorded in the book of Acts (2:41-42).[6] The disciples wor-
shiped, had fellowship, studied, and performed wonders among
the suffering. If one takes this simple structure as one among
mostly unknown possibilities, and combines some of the insights
given to us by the rock music scene, we find surprising possibilities.

The possibilities of the church of Christ being where the action
is and where people can be "pulled out" are unlimited if the
change in communication orientation is acknowledged. If the
life situation is seen for what it is—if it is seen as that which
works to dehumanize and reduce man in the process of becoming
a person—then the heritage of the past is given new light.

In the contemporary church, specialization is valued. We love
to dissect the aspects of the Christian life until there is mere
fragmentation of what was once the one body. We have worship
at one time, committee meetings at another, study at still another
time. Mission is tacked on as being separate from all else. The
rock music of today calls us to restore a wholeness to the content
and media of being the body of Christ as a basis for rebellion.

Stephen Rose has suggested a grass roots church which could
ecumenically unfold in its life mission at the local level.[7] En-
richment in each area of the Christian life could be provided by
the former separate buildings, which would become outposts for
the major tasks of the church. As attractive as this striking
blueprint for the future may be, it is presently remote from so
many communities where needed mergers within a single tradition cannot even be accomplished.

The questions facing the church are not raised just to "get
the kids into the church." The questions of criticism explicit or
implicit in the thought of rock theology are directed to the
future of the church in our times. The times have changed and
so have the people. There is no one key to unlock the power
that has been closeted from the world these long years. A pro-

cess of rebellion in the teaching and worship tasks of the church is beginning.

3. Humanistic Concerns: "People Power"

Rock music and its generation invite us to be human. We must be ready for the religious happening in worship—just as if we believed that God is with man. The church is called to respond to human need without committee meetings to decide mission. As life unfolds, the church through its people is there and spontaneously being itself.

This is not an age when the young rebel without cause. There is cause for rebellion. Both generations know it. The *other* generation plays at doing something about human justice, debating involvement in the name of Christ when there is no justification for mere words. Some people, who still remain within its body, try to fix the cracks with new ministries or some mission project among the poor. The humanity of Christ's body fails to be manifested in so much of this type of activity.

Members of the *other* generation who care about the needs of others often mistake what they need to do in order to be the body of Christ for what little they actually do for others. For example, the dedicated man tells how he enjoys his infrequent work with the poor migrants. What he does is good. He does such service to gain satisfaction. The destructive nature of this self-righteousness totally escapes him. In terms of a humanistic view of theology, he is there because he needs the poor! As James Baldwin has reminded us, the black man can be assured of his humanity, but the white man can never know his humanity.[8] Only through the forgiveness of the black man is there hope for the white man to recover his dignity.

During the wave of rioting in the summers of 1967 and 1968, it was interesting to encounter the contrasting responses from within and without the church. Church people often vented their fears by claiming that this abusive rioting was the last straw. "The poor have been fed with our good tax money and now in gratitude the slum dwellers do this kind of thing." Such a statement must be translated as meaning that the black man in frustration has dared to drive home the reality of the dehumanizing slum existence to the affluent. The black man hears such a comment of anger from the white man and knows all the more deeply that whitey remains far removed from the pain of others. "I emasculate, strangle, burn, and destroy *myself*, my home—and you have the nerve to say, 'Don't do this to *me!*' "

On the other hand, some of the most impressive, compassionate, and Christlike statements came over the mass media. A news commentator editorialized in the heat of destruction that "this is a color television problem more than a colored problem." From such a statement he continued to analyze the increasing sensitivity to the widening gap between the affluent and the poor in this age of mass media. What do the young think when they hear such a plea for a humanistic understanding and reconstruction while their Christian parents sit in the living room and moan about the low morals of those "dirty niggers"? The comfortable Christian so often demonstrates his emotional distance from humans in need when he judges the uncomfortable and suffering portion of Christ's body.

The Christian members of the *now* generation see by means of their media orientation and faith that persons are called to be where the action of serving others is because they need to discover themselves. The success of the Peace Corps program well illustrates this factor. Perceptive leaders in the corps know that America's greatest fruits from the program are what happens to the young people and older folks who are part of it. Others are helped, but the corpsmen are aided in the endless task of becoming persons.

The theological interest of this book via the *now* generation has been one which calls the church to recognize the incarnational gift that once belonged to it. There is a plea here for an awareness of the relationship between means of communication and content. The human facing the Christian gospel can only know who the person of Jesus Christ is—and is not—through his relationship with others in the task of worship, study, and service. It is the human life together which conveys this essence. The new reverence implies a new discovery of our humanity.

The age of change calls us to struggle with our personhood with others. The church must claim its true gift of Christ's humanity. Youth's discovery of the need for others in order to be fully human has freed a generation to be creative persons.

The local pastor or clergyman is badly in need of such an insight to be creatively human. Dietrich Bonhoeffer wrote on this matter from Finkenwalde, the pastoral renewal center in Nazi Germany:

> The pastor, and particularly the young pastor, suffers from being by himself. The burden of preaching is particularly heavy today for the solitary pastor who is not a prophet, but just a servant of the church.[9]

The young pastor does indeed find himself in a majority of contexts as a man in isolation. The clergy association is usually empty of real encounter and mutual ministry. Even church governmental structures often fail to provide a manifestation of the church which provides for a corporate ministry to those called to teach or preach.

For example, the isolation of a solitary ministry was crowding the lives of two suburban pastors with sourness and darkness. The small burdens of the parish ministry were elevated to a level of great perplexity. At this juncture the two pastors from nearby churches happened to cross paths. It was a rare moment and they developed a relationship beyond the usual bulletin-exchanging level. The masks were dropped and mutual fears and frustrations were shared. At first they planned to develop their own church school materials and rebuild their congregations as bastions of theological insight and Christian mission. The dreams did enable them to discover that by pooling common troubles and fantasy solutions, they were able to think creatively on the life and mission of the church. Modesty replaced the first visions. They knew that they had to start with the renewal of themselves and their work, but not in isolation.

A midweek retreat was the beginning of this fellowship of teaching and preaching. Selecting a third church building for their meeting place, they invited interested persons within their congregations to weekly sessions of study, fellowship, and worship. This was a team-teaching effort which would link media and content and challenge the concept of teaching in the two congregations.

The day a week of preparation, study, and brain-storming for the one-and-a-half hour of teaching became the high point of this work. Following a lectionary series on the book of Acts, the hours of study shed light on exciting ideas for sharing the texts with their people. Influenced by the work of the East Harlem Protestant Parish, they agreed to make Bible study, fellowship, and worship one mutual thrust. They also accepted a covenant of discipline by agreeing to preach on the same text for the Sunday worship.

The study sessions began each week with one of the two teaching ministers presenting the symbols and interpreting them. Each week the teaching leader asked the people to rise and receive the symbols of their salvation. As the sessions progressed, the symbols evolved from the Cup and Bread placed on a red handkerchief ("We use it to wipe the sweat, blood, and tears of our existence, and it is here that the gospel comes") to a broken Coke bottle and a newspaper with the news of a summer riot in Chicago ("Even in such chaos God comes and cares"). Each person then made an offering to God in the presence of his neighbor by responding to a question posed by the leader (i.e., passing a mirror from person to person and asking, "What do you see?"). The passage to be studied was then read and the rest of the evening was spent in relating the message of the text to the lives of those present. The meeting was concluded with the passing of the peace. The leader grasped the hands of his neighbor between his hands and said: "The peace of God be with you." And the person receiving the peace responded: "And with thy spirit." He then, in turn, passed the peace on.

What made this experience so rewarding for those participating was the freedom to rebel against the traditional teaching approaches of the past. Supported by the example and encouragement of Edward A. White, then Director of City Church Project of Chicago, they sought to creatively relate content and teaching method. For example, the setting for a study of Paul's conversion was created by having the teachers blindfold each participant as he or she entered the room. They were led to the table and the symbols were presented. For the next hour and a half the group responded to human situations quite beyond the usual suburban setting. A tape recording was played of a young girl's attempt to express the desperation and confusion she felt upon being released from prison after the death of her lover. "How would you respond if this were your daughter speaking?" The members of the group responded on the level of academic concern with advice on the counseling she should receive. The tape was played again and each person was asked to place his or her hands on the table. A woman who had been in the room without the knowledge of those present stopped at each person's place, took his hands in hers and said, "Help me." The earlier round of intellectual responses was suddenly replaced by deep human encounters with another person. One man stammered with great feeling, "I would put my arms around you and tell you that I love you." The touch of a person in need enabled a new level of involvement to be reached.

After sharing the burden of black people via the pen of James Baldwin and wrestling with his point that the white man needed the forgiveness of the black to recover his humanity (as Ananias needed Paul to fulfill his ministry), the ministers concluded by pausing behind each of the sitting persons to remove blindfolds with the words: "Brother [name], the Lord Jesus . . . has sent me that you may regain your sight and be filled with the Holy Spirit" (Acts 9:17). The parting question of sharing was: "What do you see now as Christians?"

Not every evening produced the same kinds of responses. No one will ever forget the great night of hostility. The group was struggling with the story of Paul's hostile reception in the marketplace. How could this text be presented so that it might be meaningful to them? The plan emerged from the cross-fertilization of a corporate ministry as teaching ministers. The group met at the host church and were told to follow the pastors in their cars. The pastors took them to the parking lot of a supermarket which was still open and very busy. They set up folding chairs in the parking lot. The small circle of Christians preparing to study was a shocking sight to the suburban shoppers. Placing a paper cup and wrapper from a hamburger stand on the blacktop as symbols, the teaching pastors started the usual study.

The class members were asked to share how they felt about being out in the world. Each member in his own way expressed anger, fear, and embarrassment at being there where all these people could give them strange stares. The rest of the experience was devoted to a struggle with Paul's hostile reception in the marketplace as a witness to Christ. Things were still a bit icy as they dismissed with the peace. During the week most of those present called one of the leaders and expressed the impact of that evening in the parking lot and the real bite of Paul's mission in the world. In some cases, words of apology were included. From this experience, the teachers were aware that this covenant ministry had the added benefit of giving the teacher courage to undertake plans even when they might lead to initial resistance. Alone either of them would have deserted the teaching plan after the first round of blistering hostility. Together, however, there was courage to continue.

It was amazing how the biblical studies kept encouraging them to rebel from the patterns of the past by using contemporary materials as teaching vehicles. Suddenly, the prophetic words of the Beatles ("Help") or Simon and Garfunkel ("Seven O'Clock News/Silent Night") joined the penetrating insights of the Elaine May and Mike Nichols comedy skits as means by which message and medium could be linked together in a chain of experience. Games, not in the sense of Eric Berne's usage but in the tradition of improvisational theater, even became vital aspects of the teaching task of the church as the two pastors now saw it. The fine line between gimmickry and creative teaching was firmly drawn through the security of disciplined study. Creativity was assured by the supportive communion between the teaching team.

The midweek experience also greatly affected their understanding of worship. Their past preaching was suddenly cast into a new light. The drama of salvation seemed to have been reduced to a mere gesture by the pastors' past efforts. They needed freedom for the Spirit to move and work. The intense study and the dialogue with their people at the midweek retreat put them in command of the sermon content as never before. The pastors felt that this preparation should enable them to communicate what was in hand. They began preaching while standing in front of the communion table without immediate reference to their carefully prepared notes.

One Sunday the sermon was introduced by the pastor carrying a huge picket sign around the communion table. He slowly repeated the slogan "Freedom now!" On another occasion, the startling power of the early preaching was vividly set before the people by the bearer of the Word standing on a wooden carton.

Taking seriously the interests and thought idioms of the people in the congregation, a certain Sunday one of the pastors proclaimed the message from a startling perspective. At the point of the worship for the sermon, the minister removed his robe, placed a large paper hat on his head, and sat before the communion table holding on his lap a drum obtained from one of the high school members who played in a local rock group. The sermon came through the character of Oskar, a creation of Günther Grass (*The Tin Drum*). The pastor beat the drum and preached from the perspective of this thirty-six-inch character. After the service a lady stopped at the door and said, "Oskar told us so much." On yet another Sunday small stones from the parking lot were handed out as the people were about to return to their seats after having partaken of the Lord's Supper. They were told that the small stones in their hands represented the price paid for the bread in their mouths. Stephen and countless others had felt the pain of literal stoning in order that others might know God's love. The stone would be a mark of the cost of their witness for Christ in the world.

There has been a delay reporting a most important part of this covenant relationship between two pastors. The community of believers within these congregations who undertook this experiment in corporate study, worship, and fellowship added the blaze of excitement to this experience of rebellion by contributing fresh ideas for worship and study. The pastors not only discovered the sin of pastoral isolation but also received the gift of a mutual ministry from God's people.

Pastor Bonhoeffer spoke not only to a Germany in agony under Nazi rule but also to the American church of the 60's when he wrote:

> [The solitary pastor] needs brotherly help and fellowship not only to show him what he is to preach, but also to show him how to preach it.[10]

From this modest experiment the two pastors saw that the beginning of renewal in the office of creative teacher and pastor must come from covenant relationships between pastor and pastor, and pastors and people.[11]

From this case study it becomes clear that the rock generation's call for humanity can be channeled to the church of our day. As Christ comforted by touch, as he taught through example, metaphor, and items familiar to his time, so is it proper for the church to break out of its hibernation and be real with real people.

4. Experiential Zest: "Morning Mouth?"

The television advertisement captures the feeling one has after a long rest but now facing another day: morning mouth. The church has a bad taste in its mouth after its long rest from the world. It is time to brush out the old and to experience a solid freshness by which the church can enable its people to face others without embarrassment.

How could a local church experience the lessons of the *now* generation? With the impact of the music and insights of youth, one can speculate about a creative teaching experience. For example, a particular church could have a short study on youth culture. A contract of time limitation will attract people more readily than the organizational structure of the past which met endlessly. Perhaps there would be eight sessions or less in which both *now* and *other* generation people could gather to study. It could be decided that rock music would lead you to a study of the *now* generation as suggested by the present study. About eight to twelve people would be found who agree to commit themselves to such a study. The idea of unity in the Christian life would be maintained.

At the beginning of the hour-and-a-half or two-hour sessions (or set a length of time agreed upon by all), "the symbols of our salvation" would be presented. To select such symbols, the leaders could let their imaginations carry the theme of Christ and common life into new and unexpected areas. Beginning with the obvious or familiar, the symbols could gradually become more demanding of understanding. This is in keeping with the experiential orientation of the rock generation. People do not need to be "led" in their thinking by the obvious or "hot" forms of media. A Bible, a cross, and a newspaper placed in the center of the table represent to all what God has done in Christ. Experimentation will make a great difference. Student-centered involvement could be stimulated when a group of blindfolded people pass a coffee cup from hand to hand or are led to a window and trace the cross made by the frame. The Christian, in such a teaching experience, encounters the reality of the message via his senses.

The visual and sensual awareness of God's gift of forgiveness and love need not be limited to items of a small nature. The very setting of the study can be altered by decor or location to make it consistent with the study. Perhaps the study group could spend an evening at a local coffee house as participants in discussion. Posters or other means of altering atmospheric aspects of the meeting area can be used to enable the students to probe the sensual nature of the study material.

The leader might also give an opportunity for each person to make an offering to God in the presence of his neighbor. Questions can be used to focus this sharing. Responses should be stimulated through open-ended questions for which there is no one right answer. Each person should be reverently asked to make a response. If a person cannot answer verbally, this must be accepted without any kind of judgment. Silence communicates something important to the sensitive.

If the church is trying experimental teaching for the first time, it is suggested that a text be selected for each week's study. For instance, every chapter in this book refers to texts, and one can easily be chosen. The text can be read and perhaps a brief exegetical comment may be made by the teaching leader.

This series of studies on youth and contemporary faith could use music from the rock poets as a major source. Several carefully selected pieces may be used for each lesson. The group will have difficulty hearing the lyrics at first. The teaching leader may write them on the board. They may not be mimeographed because of copyright laws. The leader should keep the discussion on the musical material while not directing the group to his pre-determined conclusions. The inductive or student-centered teaching is a means by which the teacher enables the students to learn by thinking.[12] After a good discussion on a song, the teacher might simply ask what relationship there is between the Scripture passage and the rock poetry. Make them work to find similarities and differences.

As master teacher Gilbert Highet reminds us,

> . . . when people laugh together, they cease to be young and old, master and pupils, workers and driver, jailer and prisoners, they become a single group of human beings enjoying its existence.[13]

Humor abounds in the rock music under study. The young laugh and find joy in their life. However, the church never seems to smile or to enjoy its existence. Laughter is one of the most powerful means by which the contemporary culture presents its philosophy to all of us. The advertisement on television which enables us to smile or laugh is remembered.

Our hypothetical study group might take the cue from the *now* generation and use humor in its experience. Some of the humorous songs noted in this study might be selected or perhaps straight comedy material from such significant sources as Nichols and May, *Second City*, Lenny Bruce, *Beyond the Fringe*, etc., might be chosen. The material must be carefully selected and have a place in the topic under discussion. Often comedy material which has real depth is hard to find. Comedy albums appear in limited quantities and are quickly gone. Sensitive teachers in the church collect such materials. A local source can be found with some inquiry.

Humor has proven to be one of the most useful ways of "pulling out" a group of studying Christians. For example, a *Second City* routine about a conversation between a social worker and Puerto Rican youth reveals in fifteen minutes the major problem of interpersonal relationships between the poor and the affluent. One study group spent two hours of serious discussion on this pathos-humor routine. It is wise to replay such material at the conclusion, or even midway through the discussion. New vistas of insight will be found by a fresh hearing of the material. The very idea of using humor in church study opens the possibility of other applications. Could not the opening round of sharing request a joke from each person in place of an answer to a question? Doesn't one reveal a great deal about himself through that which is funny to him? Or couldn't the group be asked to pair up and be assigned the task of bringing jokes which must be told in pairs for the offering period next session?

One week the major study material could be a focus on one of the teen music heroes. A collection of fan magazines could be distributed as source material. What characteristics appeal to the youth of today and why? Does this say something to the church about the image of the teen's heroes? If the group is secure and has emotional freedom, it may be invited to dance to the music of the rock world. They could, for a brief moment, experience what those of the *now* generation feel.

Films are an excellent teaching medium if they are good and well used. If the group could obtain films like *A Hard Day's Night, The Rock Revolution* (CBS Special), or a number of excellent experimental movies now readily available, then they should be used. If the film is good, justice must be done to the work of art. Study questions often hamper the mood and communication created by the film. The teacher must be sensitive and inductive in his relationship with the group concerning the film they have experienced.

The principle of dissimilar juxtaposition, placing contrasting elements side by side, can be used to good advantage in a teaching situation such as this. This principle has been best illustrated in the early television show *The Hit Parade*. The audience would watch each week to see how the producers would visually present a long-running hit. Often the familiar song would be placed in a very different context. One word in the lyric would become a jumping-off place for an imaginative new setting. Jesus also used startling or dissimilar comparisons. There is a striking response to such a method. The student must associate things not ordinarily comparable and is drawn out to think. Rock music can easily be played while dissimilar visuals are projected for the students. There are excellent filmstrips of modern art, or photography books, such as *The Family of Man*, which used with opaque projectors can create effective teaching possibilities.

The ideas of the past few pages are not shared as a gimmick catalogue. They are meant to suggest to the reader that the world of sensitivity which is so much a part of the *now* generation suggests new avenues of experiencing the Christian faith. There is no limit to this perceptual dimension to Christian theology once the creative leap of faith has been made.

The most frustrating aspect of sharing the insights of the *now* generation and its implications for the church is the plague of timidity which grips those who teach and preach. They usually smile and agree that such ideas are interesting for some "far out" congregation. However, not for us. Such a "cop out" is merely what the *now* generation has been accustomed to receiving from most of the Christian church.

It has been the contention of this study that the roots of the Christian gospel can be seen in the music, concerns, and life of today's youth. However, the church is satisfied to retain the tradition of the past hundred years in place of finding a contemporary manifestation of its real essence. Perhaps the test whether this is true or not will be seen in what the reader does on completion of this page. Will he begin his own task of hearing and listening to the *now* generation? Will he be instrumental as teacher or student in experimenting with such a study group, or will there be just more morning mouth?

Notes

EDITOR'S NOTE: Lyrics of many songs referred to could not be quoted directly because the holder of the copyright did not give permission.

CHAPTER 1. THE PROBLEM: "WHAT'S HAPPENING?"

1. Quoted in *New York Times* (August 5, 1966), p. 20.
2. *Ibid.*
3. Editorial, *America* (August 20, 1966), p. 164.
4. Dean Jerald Brauer, in American church history course at University of Chicago, 1964.
5. Dietrich Bonhoeffer, *The Way to Freedom* (New York: Harper & Row, 1966), p. 72.
6. Henry Chadwick, *Early Christian Thought and the Classic Tradition* (Oxford: Oxford University Press, 1966).
7. Marshall McLuhan, *Understanding Media* (New York: McGraw-Hill Book Company, 1964); see also the same author's graphic demonstration of his "message" in *The Medium Is the Massage* with Quentin Fiore (New York: Bantam Books, Inc., 1967).
8. Carl F. Burke, *God Is for Real, Man* (New York: Association Press, 1966), p. 94.
9. See Marshall McLuhan's letter in "Dear Playboy," *Playboy* (April 1968), pp. 18-20.
10. Jean-Paul Sartre, *The Flies, No Exit and Three Other Plays,* tr. by Stuart Gilbert (New York: Vintage Books, Inc., 1959), p. 64.
11. James A. Pike, *You and the New Morality* (New York: Harper & Row, 1967), p. 70.
12. Nat Hentoff, "Profiles: The Cracklin', Shakin', Breakin' Sounds," *New Yorker* (October 24, 1964), p. 83.
13. F. J. F. Jackson, *The History of the Christian Church: From the Earliest Times to A.D. 461* (London: George Allen & Unwin Ltd., 1957), p. 301.
14. Leonard Gross, "John Lennon: Beatle on His Own," *Look* (December 13, 1966), p. 70.
15. See the half-mock, half-serious genealogy of rock music in *Cheetah* (February 1968), pp. 59-61.
16. Robert Christgau, "Rock lyrics are poetry (maybe)," *Cheetah* (December 1967), pp. 38-45, 93-95. This critic makes the distinction between poets and Bards. He places good rock music writers under the heading of "Bard" or popular poets who reach the people.
17. Nat Hentoff, "Playboy Interview: Bob Dylan," *Playboy* (March 1966), p. 44.
18. George Orwell (Eric Blair), "Inside the Whale," *A Collection of Essays* (Garden City, N. Y.: Doubleday Anchor Books, 1964), p. 218.

19. See *New York Times* reports: June 12, 1965, p. 1; June 13, 1965, p. 3; June 15, 1965, p. 15; June 16, 1965, p. 13; June 17, 1965, p. 3; June 20, 1965, p. 5.

20. John Lennon, *In His Own Write* (New York: Simon and Schuster, 1964); *A Spaniard in the Works* (New York: Simon and Schuster, 1965).

21. Peter Schickele, "About the Awful," *Nation* (June 8, 1964), pp. 588 f.

22. Vance Packard, "Building the Beatle Image," *Saturday Evening Post* (March 21, 1964), p. 36.

23. *Ibid.*

24. Thomas Meehan, "Public Writer No. 1?" *New York Times* Magazine (December 12, 1965), pp. 44 f.

25. Stephen Rose, "Bob Dylan as Theologian," *Renewal* (October-November 1965), pp. 4-7.

26. Stephen Kanfer, "Two Fine Rockers Roll Their Own," *Life* (April 21, 1967), p. 18.

27. Quoted in "Talk of the Town," *New Yorker* (January 6, 1968), p. 21.

28. The author is greatly indebted to Dr. Y. David Kim, who kindly shared his brief notes of the pre-Assembly Conference on Evangelism for delegates to the 179th General Assembly of the United Presbyterian Church in the United States of America (1967). In some cases liberties have been taken with the materials as they came into this writer's hands.

CHAPTER 2. THE IRREVERENT GENERATION: "BAN THE BIBLE"

1. *Webster's Third New International Dictionary of the English Language Unabridged,* ed. Philip Babcock Gove (Springfield, Mass.: G. & C. Merriam Company, 1961), p. 1942.

2. See Harvey Cox, *The Secular City* (New York: The Macmillan Company, 1965).

3. Sartre, *op. cit.,* p. 75.

4. Gross, *op. cit.,* p. 66.

5. "Eleanor Rigby," Copyright © 1966 Northern Songs, Ltd. 71-75 New Oxford St., London, W.C.1, Eng. All rights reserved. Used by permission

6. *Ibid.*

7. Statement made on the *Tonight Show* (July 19, 1967).

8. "Mike Nichols and Elaine May," Mercury Records (OCM 2200).

9. Anne Frank, *Anne Frank: The Diary of a Young Girl* (New York: Pocket Books, Inc., 1952), pp. 68-69.

10. "She's Leaving Home," Copyright © 1967 Northern Songs, Ltd. 71-75 New Oxford St., London, W.C.1, Eng. All rights reserved. Used by permission.

11. Used by permission. "Janey's Blues," copyright 1967—Dialogue Music, Inc.

12. Used by permission. "Hair of Spun Gold," copyright 1965—Dialogue Music, Inc.

13. *Ibid.*

14. *Ibid.*

15. Used by permission. "(Too Old To) Go 'Way Little Girl," copyright 1966—Dialogue Music, Inc.

16. Used by permission. "Society's Child," copyright 1966—Dialogue Music, Inc.

17. "Your Mother Should Know," Copyright © 1967 Northern Songs, Ltd. 71-75 New Oxford St., London, W.C.1, Eng. All rights reserved. Used by permission.

18. "The Confession of 1967," *The Book of Confessions*, 9.45 (The Office of the General Assembly of the United Presbyterian Church, U.S.A., 1966, 1967).

CHAPTER 3. THE HUMANISTIC GENERATION: "MAN ALIVE!"

1. Ben Reade, "An Easter Happening," *Renewal* (May-June 1966), pp. 3-5.

2. Sartre, *op. cit.*, p. 103.

3. Lenny Bruce, *How to Talk Dirty and Influence People* (Chicago: Playboy Press, 1967), p. 73.

4. Gross, *op. cit.*, p. 66.

5. Denis de Rougemont, *Love in the Western World* (Garden City, N. Y.: Doubleday Anchor Books, 1967), pp. 67-68.

6. Andreas Capellanus, "The Rules of Courtly Love," quoted in *The Portable Medieval Reader*, ed. by James Bruce Ross and Mary Martin McLaughlin (New York: The Viking Press, 1949), pp. 116-117.

7. Mike Nichols and Elaine May, "An Evening with Mike Nichols and Elaine May," OCM 2200 Mercury.

8. Emma Shiefman, "The Beatles? Yeah! Yeah! Yeah!" *The Reading Teacher* (October 1965), pp. 31-34.

9. Marshall McLuhan and George B. Leonard, "The Future of Sex," *Look* (July 25, 1967), pp. 56-63.

10. "For No One," Copyright © 1966 Northern Songs, Ltd. 71-75 New Oxford St., London, W.C.1, Eng. All rights reserved. Used by permission.

11. "With a Little Help from My Friends," Copyright © 1967 Northern Songs, Ltd. 71-75 New Oxford St., London, W.C.1, Eng. All rights reserved. Used by permission.

12. "Within You Without You," Copyright © 1967 Northern Songs, Ltd. 71-75 New Oxford St., London, W.C.1, Eng. All rights reserved. Used by permission.

13. See Joseph Haroutunian, *God With Us: A Theology of Transpersonal Life* (Philadelphia: The Westminster Press, 1965), or Dietrich Bonhoeffer, *Life Together* (New York: Harper & Row, 1954).

14. O. Hobart Mowrer, *The New Group Therapy* (Princeton, N. J.: D. Van Nostrand Company, Inc., 1964), pp. 65-71.

15. Günther Grass, *The Tin Drum* (Greenwich, Conn.: Fawcett Publications, Inc., 1959), pp. 506-507.

16. "The Sound of Silence," by Paul Simon © 1964 & 1965 by Charing Cross Music. Used with permission of the publisher.

17. *Ibid.*

18. *Ibid.*

19. "The Dangling Conversation," by Paul Simon © 1966 by Charing Cross Music Co. Used with permission of the publisher.

20. *Ibid.*

21. "Fixing a Hole," Copyright © 1967 Northern Songs, Ltd. 71-75 New Oxford St., London, W.C.1, Eng. All rights reserved. Used by permission.

22. Jean-Paul Sartre, *Being and Nothingness* (New York: Philosophical Society, 1956), pp. 254 ff.

23. "I Am a Rock," by Paul Simon © 1966 by Charing Cross Music. Used with permission of the publisher.

24. *Ibid.*

25. "Help," Copyright © 1967 Northern Songs, Ltd. 71-75 New Oxford St., London, W.C.1, Eng. All rights reserved. Used by permission.

26. *Ibid.*

27. "A Day in the Life," Copyright © 1965 Northern Songs, Ltd. 71-75 New Oxford St., London, W.C.1, Eng. All rights reserved. Used by permission.

28. Used by permission. "Insanity Comes Quietly to the Structured Mind," copyright 1967—Dialogue Music, Inc.

29. "With a Little Help from My Friends," Copyright © 1967 Northern Songs, Ltd. 71-75 New Oxford St., London, W.C.1, Eng. All rights reserved. Used by permission.

30. Dietrich Bonhoeffer, *Letters and Papers from Prison* (New York: The Macmillan Company, 1953), pp. 237-238.

31. "Good Day Sunshine," Copyright © 1966 Northern Songs, Ltd. 71-75 New Oxford St., London, W.C.1, Eng. All rights reserved. Used by permission.

32. "Lucy in the Sky with Diamonds," Copyright © 1967 Northern Songs, Ltd. 71-75 New Oxford St., London, W.C.1, Eng. All rights reserved. Used by permission.

33. *Ibid.*

34. "Within You Without You," Copyright © 1967 Northern Songs, Ltd. 71-75 New Oxford St., London, W.C.1, Eng. All rights reserved. Used by permission.

CHAPTER 4. THE EXPERIENTIAL GENERATION:
"UNLESS I SEE . . . PLACE MY FINGER . . . AND PLACE MY HAND . . ."

1. Ernest Hemingway, *A Moveable Feast* (New York: Bantam Books, 1965), p. 69.

2. Nat Hentoff, "Profiles: The Crackin', Shakin', Breakin' Sounds," *op. cit.*, p. 86.

3. "Ring Around-a-Rosy Rag" by Arlo Guthrie. © Copyright 1967 by Appleseed Music Inc. All Rights Reserved. Used by permission.

4. Ignatius, "Ignatius to the Ephesians," *The Apostolic Fathers* (Transcript Kirsopp Lake, Cambridge, Mass.: Harvard University Press, 1959), 20, 2, pp. 194-195.

5. "Lucy in the Sky with Diamonds," Copyright © 1967 Northern Songs, Ltd. 71-75 New Oxford St., London, W.C.1, Eng. All rights reserved. Used by permission.

6. Richard Rubenstein, "Dialogue on the New Theology and the New Morality," *After Auschwitz* (New York: Bobbs-Merrill Company, 1966), pp. 266-287.

CHAPTER 5. THE ANTI-WORK GENERATION:
"WHAT DO YOU WANT TO DO?" "NOTHING!"

1. Ralph Ellison, *Invisible Man* (New York: Random House, 1952), p. 165.

2. Leo Tolstoy, *Anna Karenina*, tr. by Constance Garnett, ed. by Leonard J. Kent and Nina Berberova (New York: The Modern Library, 1965), p. 267.

3. Paul Goodman, *Growing Up Absurd* (New York: Vintage Books, 1960), pp. 16 f.

4. Bruce, *op. cit.,* p. 81.

5. Henry C. Wallich, "Campus and Business," *Newsweek* (December 26, 1966), p. 67.

6. Dietrich Bonhoeffer, *Ethics,* ed. by Eberhard Bethge (New York: The Macmillan Company, 1955), p. 223.

7. Ray Sons, "They Make Book on Disaster," *Chicago Daily News* (December 14, 1964), section 4, p. 45.

8. "The Motorcycle Song," by Arlo Guthrie. © Copyright 1967 by Appleseed Music Inc. All Rights Reserved. Used by permission.

9. "A Hard Day's Night," Copyright © 1964 Northern Songs, Ltd. 71-75 New Oxford St., London, W.C.1, Eng. All rights reserved. Used by permission.

10. "Lovely Rita," Copyright © 1967 Northern Songs, Ltd. 71-75 New Oxford St., London, W.C.1, Eng. All rights reserved. Used by permission.

11. "Taxman," Copyright © 1966 Northern Songs, Ltd. 71-75 New Oxford St., London, W.C.1, Eng. All rights reserved. Used by permission.

12. "Paperback Writer," Copyright © 1966 Northern Songs, Ltd. 71-75 New Oxford St., London, W.C.1, Eng. All rights reserved. Used by permission.

13. "Eleanor Rigby," Copyright © 1966 Northern Songs, Ltd. 71-75 New Oxford St., London, W.C.1, Eng. All rights reserved. Used by permission.

CHAPTER 6. THE ANTI-WAR GENERATION: "KILL FOR PEACE"

1. "Kill for Peace" (Tuli Kupferberg), 1966 by United International (ASCAP). Used by permission of ESP-Disk.

2. Eric Berne, *Games People Play* (New York: Grove Press, Inc., 1964), p. 48.

3. According to *Report of the National Advisory Commission on Civil Disorders* (New York: Bantam Books, 1968), there were 14,000 rat bites reported in 1965. Most of them occurred in the slum areas of our cities (p. 273).

4. Used by permission. "Bahimsa," copyright 1968—Dialogue Music, Inc.

5. Used by permission. "Honey D'Ya Think," copyright 1968—Dialogue Music, Inc.

CHAPTER 7. YOUTH'S REBELLION AGAINST SOCIETY:
　"THESE MEN WHO HAVE TURNED THE WORLD UPSIDE DOWN . . ."

1. "Scratch a lover and find a foe," Dorothy Parker as quoted in *A Treasury of Jewish Quotations*, ed. by Joseph L. Baron (New York: Crown, 1956), p. 286.
2. "Getting Better," Copyright © 1967 Northern Songs, Ltd. 71-75 New Oxford St., London, W.C.1, Eng. All rights reserved. Used by permission
3. "When I'm Sixty-Four," Copyright © 1967 Northern Songs, Ltd. 71-75 New Oxford St., London, W.C.1, Eng. All rights reserved. Used by permission.
4. Nat Hentoff, "Playboy Interview: Bob Dylan," *op. cit.*, p. 42.
5. See Robert Reisner, *Graffiti* (New York: Parallax Publishing Company, Inc., 1967)
6. "The Sound of Silence," by Paul Simon © 1964 & 1965 by Charing Cross Music. Used with permission of the publisher.
7. Used by permission. "New Christ Cardiac Hero," copyright 1967—Dialogue Music, Inc.
8. "At the Zoo," by Paul Simon © 1967 by Paul Simon. Used with permission of the publisher.
9. Used by permission. "Society's Child," copyright 1966—Dialogue Music, Inc.
10. "I'm Going Home," by Arlo Guthrie. © Copyright 1967 by Appleseed Music Inc. All Rights Reserved. Used by permission.

CHAPTER 8. SOME PERSONAL AFTERTHOUGHTS:
　"SURELY THIS IS NOT WITHOUT MEANING . . ."

1. Orwell, "Marrekech," *op. cit.*, p. 193.
2. The Reverend David O. Barstow shared in this creative worship experience with the author.
3. The Reverend Duane Holme has done extensive experimentation to make liturgy contemporary in idiom and traditional in content.
4. Alan Paton, *Cry, the Beloved Country* (New York: Charles Scribner's Sons, 1948), p. 36.
5. Locke Bowman, *Straight Talk about Teaching in Today's Church* (Philadelphia: The Westminster Press, 1967), pp. 74-75.
6. George W. Webber, *God's Colony in Man's World* (New York: Abingdon Press, 1960), pp. 63 ff.
7. Stephen C. Rose, *The Grass Roots Church: A Manifesto for Protestant Renewal* (New York: Holt, Rinehart and Winston, Inc., 1966).
8. James Baldwin, "My Dungeon Shook: Letter to My Nephew on the One Hundredth Anniversary of the Emancipation," *The Fire Next Time* (New York: Dell Publishing Co., 1963), p. 22.
9. Bonhoeffer, *The Way to Freedom, op. cit.*, p. 30.
10. *Ibid.*

11. Portions of this report were published in the August 1967 issue of *Monday Morning*.

12. Doris J. Hill, *Teaching: the inside story* (Philadelphia: Board of Christian Education, the United Presbyterian Church, U.S.A., 1967).

13. Gilbert Highet, *The Art of Teaching* (New York: Vintage Books, 1950), p. 55.

The Author

Meet Dennis Benson. He's very big on music. Particularly rock music. "Everyone gets something different out of it," he says. "Music is an extension of people," and that's what he talks about in *The Now Generation*.

He's also big on coffee houses. He managed the Salt Cellar while he was Director of Religious Life at Waynesburg College and currently acts as consultant to a number of coffee houses in the Pittsburgh area. He is host of *The Place*, a coffee house program aired over WQED-TV, Pittsburgh.

"My background is kind of diverse," says Benson. He has been a hospital chaplain, suburban pastor, lecturer in New Testament Greek, worker in an industrial ministry, researcher for an OEO project, civil rights activist, youth adviser at several churches, and is now Director of Youth Ministry for the Council of Churches of the Pittsburgh Area.

The author received his B.A. from the University of Michigan in 1958, his B.D. from McCormick Theological Seminary in 1962, then did three years' graduate work at the University of Chicago. His wife, Marilyn, is a schoolteacher, and they have two daughters, Amy and Jill.